GEORGE WOODCOCK'S
INTRODUCTION TO
CANADIAN FICTION

George Woodcock

※

GEORGE WOODCOCK'S INTRODUCTION TO CANADIAN FICTION

ECW PRESS

CANADIAN CATALOGUING IN PUBLICATION DATA

Woodcock, George, 1912–
  George Woodcock's Introduction to Canadian fiction

Includes bibliographical references and index.
ISBN 1-55022-141-8

1. Canadian fiction (English) — History and criticism*
I. Title. II Title: Introduction to Canadian fiction.

PS8187.W65 1993   C813.009   C91-095030-X
PR9192.2.W65 1993

George Woodcock's Introduction to Canadian Fiction has been published with the assistance of grants from The Canada Council and the Ontario Arts Council.

Design and imaging by ECW Type & Art, Oakville, Ontario.
Printed and bound by Hignell Printing Limited, Winnipeg, Manitoba.

Distributed by General Publishing Co. Limited, 30 Lesmill Road, Toronto, Ontario M3B 2T6.

Published by ECW PRESS, 1980 Queen Street East, Toronto, Ontario M4L 1J2.

CONTENTS

Introduction

A DECADE AGO — give a year either way — Jack David and Robert Lecker of ECW PRESS approached me with a very ambitious project. I had already contributed to the press's parent journal, *Essays on Canadian Writing*, and had written introductions to one or two of its books. But this was something much larger. When the *Literary History of Canada* appeared in 1965 many people remarked that — now we had the descriptive material of the *History* — we needed a more analytical work to complement it, a broad critical survey of Canadian writing from its beginnings. This, to all intents and purposes, was what Jack David and his associates Robert Lecker and Ellen Quigley were proposing. They planned to involve somewhere between eighty and a hundred critics in a twenty-volume oeuvre that would cover Canadian fiction and poetry for the past two centuries since the earliest garrison and pioneer writers. It was to be called *Canadian Writers and Their Works*.

It would be a work with deliberately imposed limitations. Only books in English would find a place, and rich areas of even English-Canadian writing — exploration and biography, history and criticism, and the general essay — would be ignored, at least for the time being. And to enable fullness of consideration, the editors would abandon the broad-net approach of the *Literary History*, which sought to name at least every minnow in the literary pond, and strike for the big fish in long essays about individual writers. Round about fifty poets and fifty fiction writers were chosen and arranged in rough groups that tended to emphasize both period and various forms of affinity. The whole work would reach almost six thousand pages, and the individual essays would be long enough for publication as separate monographs.

Jack David's suggestion was that I write a "unifying intro-duction" to each of the volumes. He and his associates aimed at that time to print the final volumes in 1990; in fact they have published them in 1992. Their timetable would give me the greater part of the 1980s to write twenty substantial essays, as well as all the other work I customarily undertake, but since it was related to my abiding interest in Canadian writing, it seemed an extension of my current work rather that an extra burden, and I agreed.

So we started, the editors gathering the essays, I writing the introductions as soon as the pieces had been assembled and edited for each volume, and proceeded by a leapfrog process, the first volumes appearing in 1983, my final introduction being written in the summer of 1991, and the last volumes appearing in the following year. Owing to the extreme decentralization of the Canadian literary community — and perhaps also to my own reclusive tendencies — Jack David and I did not meet until the end of our common task when, all volumes assembled and all introductions written, we sat down in Vancouver to drink a crock of wine and eat a meal together.

What I realized as I got to work was that my task of unification was proceeding on a double level; not merely did the introductions bring together the writers discussed in their respective volumes, but a kind of unified panorama of Canadian writing was being revealed stage by stage as they were completed. About halfway through the project the editors and I came to the conclusion that my pieces, in introducing the various essays, were in fact developing a personal view of Canadian writing that was worth preserving for its own sake. And well before the time all the tasks connected with *Canadian Writers and Their Works* were individually completed, we all agreed on the feasibility of the present two volumes — one representing my personal view of the development of Canadian poetry and the other my personal view of the development of Canadian fiction since the early days of the genre in this country.

This is the volume on fiction. The various chapters correspond roughly to the various introductions, but in fitting them to a new format certain adjustments have seemed necessary. Some writers not originally listed have produced work that makes them appear a great deal more important than they were a decade ago; Timothy Findley is a case in point. Others were omitted from the beginning, but they deserve attention; examples are that early satirist from the Maritimes, Thomas McCulloch, and that pioneer experimental modernist, Howard O'Hagan. In these cases, I have inserted appropriate passages discussing the writers and relating them to their contemporaries. Writers who have continued working after the essays on them in *Canadian Writers and Their Works* was completed constitute another problem; I have solved this by adding to my comments only in cases where the more recent work seems to demand an important reassessment of the writer's oeuvre. Examples are Mordecai Richler, whose *Solomon Gursky Was Here* seemed to reverse strikingly a downward curve I had observed in the force of his writing; and Margaret Atwood, who continually surprises one, as she has done most recently in *Cat's Eye* by the novelty and clarity of her perceptions. An example of another kind is that of Matt Cohen on whom my comments in the original volume where he was discussed were scanty because I had written the actual essay on him; I have now summarized more fully both his earlier novels of the decadent rural society of Salem in the country north of Kingston and his later books with their more cosmopolitan themes and settings.

CHAPTER I

Pioneers and Garrisons: Frances Brooke, John Richardson, Rosanna Leprohon, Susanna Moodie, and Others

THERE IS SOMETHING of the fascination of a Darwinian exercise about tracing the origins of a national culture or a national literature. When does a variation become so distinctive and enduring that we must call it a new species? Or, to transfer this idea into the spatial-temporal terms of a culture emerging in a young country, when does a new place create a new voice?

One can put the question in another way by asking whether American literature begins with Captain John Smith's *True Relations of . . . Virginia* (1608), a vigorously written account of the first settlement in what is now the United States, or with, say, Charles Brockden Brown's *Wieland*, which was written at the end of the eighteenth century and is the ancestor of a notable Gothic strain in American fiction running through Poe and Hawthorne down to Faulkner and other Southern novelists in our own day. (It is also, incidentally, something of an ancestor of at least one of the writers discussed in this essay for John Richardson, when he wrote *Wacousta*, can hardly have been unaware of *Wieland* or of Brown's powerful and horrific novel of Indian wars in the American wilderness, *Edgar Huntly*.)

I think we would have to take Brown as our benchmark, for Smith was writing for English people the narrative of an English venture in the Americas which did not survive to become part of the fabric of American society, while Brown, though he was working in a literary mode derived from Europe and particularly from the English Gothic strain represented by William Godwin, was using an American setting and American people (natives and immigrants) and, above all, writing for a developing American literary public. Yet the selection of Brown does not mean the rejection of Smith; for, though it is impossible to describe Smith as an American writer in the sense of his having helped to develop an American literary consciousness, the *True Relations of . . . Virginia* is a contribution to our knowledge of what America *was*. In the same way, the narratives of the early attempts to navigate the North West Passage or of early Hudson's Bay Company wanderers like Kelsey and Henday are contributions to our knowledge of what the land that became Canada was, without being legitimately part of Canadian literature as it eventually emerged.

In other words, there is literature that is *about* a country without being *of* it (D.H. Lawrence's splendid travel books on Mexico and Italy spring to mind as brilliant examples); and there is literature that — whatever its setting may be — is beyond doubt *of* its author's country (and, in this case, Margaret Laurence's *The Prophet's Camel Bell* and her African fictions are equally good examples).

In the writers discussed here, it seems to me, we have an interesting progression, from literature about a country but not of it, through pioneer literature that is of the country in the sense of having found its place without finding its true voice, to the critical point when, to use a chemical analogy, the new voice is about to liquefy and become perceptible.

Carole Gerson, writing on the mid-nineteenth-century trio of Leprohon, Machar, and De Mille,[1] remarks that they "had little sense of belonging to a national literary movement" and that until the 1890s ". . . nearly all Canadian poets and novelists . . . suffered the absence of a stimulating, self-critical artistic community transcending civil and provincial boundaries." One might even go further and say that such a "self-critical artistic community" has really emerged in Canada — at least in a literary context — only during the past half-century, beginning with the emergence of the *New Provinces* poets in the 1930s, with their critical acuity and their historical intuitions.

Yet, as Gerson adds, "In the case of Leprohon, De Mille, and Machar, a combination of choice and chance shaped their literary fortunes, destining them to support their country's conservative cultural values and to refrain from challenging the limits of their own talents." And it is here, it seems to me, in recognizing limitations, both personal and cultural, that the kind of consciousness which creates a "national literary movement" begins to emerge, for limitations define, and out of self-definition emerges an awareness of possibilities and their creative development. In other words, we have reached, with novelists like these three, the point when writers are about to speak in the new voice of a culture defining itself, as their immediate successors like Isabella Valancy Crawford and Sara Jeannette Duncan certainly do.

Frances Brooke, in *The History of Emily Montague*, clearly wrote about Canada but is not of Canada; she is the first of a brilliant series of birds of passage and as such belongs to Canada's literary history rather than to the Canadian literary tradition. This does not mean that she is without interest to us; on the contrary, she is of greater interest since she represents a kind of literary intelligence that has often appeared among us — observing, providing data, congealing perceptions into images that remain and affect our culture even when the writer, who is never quite one of us, has departed. In a largely immigrant culture in the process of formation, the temporarily resident wanderer plays a much more welcome role than he does in the established cultures, where he always remains the outsider, a kind of itinerant trader who will carry back to his homeland the treasures of observation he has gathered but leave nothing the natives value behind him. One can compare Canadians like Mavis Gallant and Norman Levine, living out their writing lives expatriately without arousing much awareness or wielding much influence in the countries they have chosen (France and England respectively), with the long succession of writers from Frances Brooke, through Anna Jameson and Patrick Anderson and Malcolm Lowry, down to Brian Moore in our own day, who have lived for a few years or months among us and revealed us in the mirrors of their consciousnesses; such writers have influenced not only our views of ourselves but also our ways of expressing them, and their place in our cultural history is unassailable, even if it would be foolish to lay claim to them as Canadian writers.

Frances Brooke's *The History of Emily Montague* shows the special influence of its Canadian ambience by being, as James Talman and Ruth Talman pointed out in *Literary History of*

Canada, much less dominated by violated action than most of the eighteenth-century English novels of sensibility among which it belongs:

> Its sensation is provided by its setting: Canadian forests and rivers, Indians and habitants, waterfalls and snows. Is it a novel only, or might it be classed also with description and travel literature?[2]

The last sentence contains a very interesting suggestion, which I shall take up later. In the meantime, it is worth remarking on the ambivalence of Frances Brooke's attitude — or that of her characters — to the setting in which their relationships frustratingly entangle. The splendours of scenery are described in terms of conventional pre-Romantic admiration; the rigours of winter are seen in harsher terms, so that there are times when *Roughing It in the Garrison* would seem an appropriate enough alternative title for *The History of Emily Montague*. Consider a passage like this:

> I must venture to Quebec to-morrow, or have company at home: amusements are here necessary to life; we must be jovial, or the blood will freeze in our veins.
> I no longer wonder the elegant arts are unknown here; the rigour of the climate suspends the very powers of the understanding; what then must become of those of the imagination? Those who expect to see
> "A new Athens rising near the pole,"
> will find themselves extremely disappointed. Genius will never mount high, where the faculties of the mind are benumbed half the year.[3]

A worthy predecessor of Susanna Moodie speaks here. And *Emily Montague*, for all its occasional toying with the idea of a Canada transformed by "every elegant art" into something like an English landscape designed by Humphry Repton, with neat gardens and "enamelled meadows," ends in a note of rejection — and specifically rejection of the setting — when the bright and coquettish Bell half flippantly and half sadly remarks as she prepares to depart for England:

Not but this is a divine country, and our farm a terrestrial paradise; but we have lived in it almost a year, and one grows tired of every thing in time, you know . . . (III, 143)

Emily Montague is indeed virtually unique among the English eighteenth-century novels of sensibility in the way it gives depth to its rendering of a little garrison society in a provincial capital by a vivid use of the physical setting as something much more than background; yet, in doing this, it reminds me of the work of a woman writer of the preceding century who also visited a British colony and wrote a novel about it. The novel is Aphra Behn's *Oroonoko; or, The Royal Slave* (1688), set in Surinam, where Behn lived for a while as Brooke did in Quebec, and resembling *Emily Montague* in the way its vivid descriptions of an exotic environment are used to set and maintain a tone. But *Oroonoko*, with its presentation of the cruelties of slavery and the corruptness of colonial systems, is a far darker novel than *Emily Montague*, and if there is a point at which Behn's acerbic tone finds an echo among the writers discussed in this volume, it is in the sharper prose and the mordant character sketches of Susanna Moodie, whose pre-Victorian evangelical Christianity would, of course, have been deeply offended by Behn's Restoration amoralism.

But perhaps the most valid reason for evoking the ghost of Aphra Behn, the first woman to become a professional writer, is that of the seven authors discussed in this volume no less than five are women. All of them were perhaps not professional, in the sense of earning their entire livings from writing, but all of them were dedicated and persistent writers, and all of them, except Susanna Moodie, continued writing to the end of what were, in some cases, very long lives; Catharine Parr Traill lived to be ninety-seven and Agnes Maule Machar to be ninety.

The exceptional importance of women writers in Canada is a phenomenon that has become especially noticeable in recent decades, but it is striking to find the situation already present in the early years of our culture. True, the list of men writers might have been filled out with the inclusion of Joseph Howe, Thomas McCulloch, and similar names, but the dominance of women writers in this formative stage of the Canadian literary tradition would still have been evident.

In the case of women engaged in the pioneer settlement of the land, like Moodie and Traill, one can perhaps offer as an explanation — or a partial one — the fact that their menfolk were too rigorously bound to the toil the land demanded, and it is true that after a lifetime of hard work, Samuel Strickland, the brother of the two ladies, only proved himself a member of the writing Stricklands twenty-nine years after his arrival by publishing his memoirs of pioneer living in Upper Canada. But Frances Brooke, Rosanna Leprohon, and Agnes Machar all belonged to cultured urban families. That they embarked on literary careers, and persisted in them with such strength of will, suggests a freedom of manners in early Canadian society, despite its Methodistical or Jansenist moralism, which encouraged such free enterprise in artistic terms among women of talent.

Of course, it would distort the picture these literary careers represent if one were to think of all of them as wholly Canadian. Frances Brooke went back to England in 1768 after five years — interrupted by a long trip home — in Canada. The memory of her North American experiences doubtless lingered; an anonymous novel about Canada, *All's Right at Last; or, The History of Miss West*, has with some plausibility been attributed to her. How widely *Emily Montague* was remembered or read in Canada during the generations following publication, it is hard to tell; ninety-eight years after it appeared, as Lorraine McMullen tells,[4] it was noticed by Henry Morgan in his *Bibliotheca Canadensis* (1867), but it was not for another sixty years, in the 1920s, that the first serious consideration was given to the book by Canadian critics.

As for Frances Brooke, she slipped back into the London literary world like a trout returned to the water and was involved in writing and theatrical production until her death in 1789, the year when the French Revolution brought an end to her neo-Augustan world. Certainly she was a literary figure of modest standing, well known enough to earn the resentment of David Garrick, the amused acceptance of Fanny Burney, and the acquaintanceship of Samuel Johnson. Her status in the "Johnson circle" is unclear, and it would perhaps be taking things too far to talk of friendship. For there was a curious story about Brooke and Johnson. She is said to have asked him to read some of her plays, at the same time boasting of all her literary "irons in the fire." Pestered for a comment, Johnson irascibly replied: "Tell Mrs. Brooke she should put her plays where she keeps her irons!"

The Strickland sisters, Susanna Moodie and Catharine Parr Traill, belonged to a well-known English mid-nineteenth-century literary family. Along with three other of their five sisters, they had started writing in their teens as an elegant accomplishment and had kept it up for money when their father died and the family funds ran low. Catharine's first book, *The Tell Tale*, appeared when she was sixteen; Susanna, after early children's stories like *Spartacus*, which appeared when she was nineteen, published sketches and poems in *La Belle Assemblée*, a court and fashion magazine, when she was twenty-four. Both thus had modest literary careers by the time they sailed for Canada, and they went there with every intention of writing about their experiences. One of their sisters, Agnes, gained a considerable standing in the English literary world as a result of her many-volumed *Lives of the Queens of England*, and the best-known works of the two Canadian Strickland sisters, Catharine's *The Backwoods of Canada* and Susanna's *Roughing It in the Bush*, were written primarily with an eye to English readers, telling them about the strange and alien world of the Canadian pioneers. It was only when time made that world strange and alien to us also that *The Backwoods* and *Roughing It* became Canadian classics; by then, they had long been forgotten in England.

Yet — and this is one of the most important things about them — the Strickland sisters did not seek merely to be expatriates writing for English readers. They had committed their lives to Canada, sealing that commitment by years of hardship. Both endeavoured, with moderate success, to make careers as Canadian writers, involving themselves in whatever magazines appeared in the upper and lower colonies, it being too soon for Canadian publishing to offer them much opportunity to bring out their books locally.

In the case of the Strickland sisters, one sees the parallels between the pioneering life, as such, and the pioneering of a literary culture. The pioneer when he arrives in a new land has no model but the old land he left behind him. What he seeks to do, as Ed Rivers dreamed of doing in *Emily Montague*, is to create in the wilderness a kind of paradise free from the restrictions of his past world, yet retaining its essential order. The Moodies, the Traills, and their kind all sought to do this, yet the materials from which they had to

7

make their new life, including the wilderness that would be its site, were all new and different. This was why the literary myth of Robinson Crusoe, a self-made man living a self-made life on a deserted island, so fascinated them. Traill was especially attracted to it, calling one of her Canadian novels *The Canadian Crusoes: A Tale of the Rice Lake Plains* and remarking in *The Backwoods of Canada*:

> We begin to get reconciled to our Robinson Crusoe sort of life, and the consideration that the present evils are but temporary, goes a great way towards reconciling us to them.[5]

But, as even Robinson Crusoe discovered, no wilderness is proof from intrusion, and every Canadian pioneer found the land inhabited by people of other cultures with whom conflict was possible, whether they were John Richardson's Indians, Susanna Moodie's Yankees, or the French, whose relationship with the English invaders forms part of the substance of *Emily Montague* and most of the substance of Rosanna Leprohon's *Antoinette de Mirecourt; or, Secret Marrying and Secret Sorrowing*.

One can deal with such a situation in a number of ways, and the approaches writers from Brooke to Leprohon use reveal the links between the way people lived in Canada during this formative period of our culture and the literature that emerged from it. For, as Dennis Duffy in his essay on John Richardson notes:

> We ignore at our peril the actual, as opposed to the imaginative, experiences any writer undergoes. When one of those experiences is a war fought at the impressionable age of sixteen, we must acknowledge those aspects of the conflict that reverberate throughout an author's work.[6]

And there are other kinds of conflict than war.

Perhaps they come together most clearly in the concept of the garrison, first observed by Northrop Frye and since then, largely through the influence of Margaret Atwood's *Survival*, given what often seems a disproportionate importance in Canadian writing generally considered. Yet the garrison is, of course, central to John Richardson's Canadian novels, and especially to *Wacousta*, where the fortress of Detroit is the centre of an action based on defence and penetration; even though the garrison itself may be preserved, it provides no shelter for doomed individuals.

The garrison in *Emily Montague* is not visibly threatened, and no major disruptions occur in the lives of the characters through the contact between the conquerors and the conquered, as happens in *Antoinette de Mirecourt*. Yet both the *canadiens* and the Indians are used in such a way as to pose a criticism of English life: a criticism which centres on the comparative status of women, and here perhaps the salient factor lies in the correction of first impressions, the realization that strange things are not necessarily so fine as their unfamiliarity may make them seem at first sight. Encountering a company of wandering Indian women, Bell enthusiastically cries: ". . . they talk of French husbands, but commend me to an Indian one, who lets his wife ramble five hundred miles, without asking where she is going" (1, 102). But very soon she learns that the apparently free life of the Indian woman has its own constraints:

> I admire their talking of the liberty of savages; in the most essential point, they are slaves: the mothers marry their children without ever consulting their inclinations, and they are obliged to submit to this foolish tyranny. (1, 116)

But Brooke, a visitor rather than a resident, always puts her English characters in the position of observers when they relate to *canadiens* and Indians. In the experience of writers who committed themselves more deeply to life in Canada, the contacts became deeper, and their resolution led in one of two directions, towards reconciliation or towards conflict.

Conflict appears at its most melodramatic in *Wacousta*, even more than in John Richardson's other writings. The background to the action is the savage war waged against the whites by Pontiac and his Indians in 1763–64, and the famous massacre of the garrison at Michilimackinac is one of the book's set pieces. But within that action there is the titanic conflict between the fake Indian Wacousta and the commander of Detroit, Colonel de Haldimar, which ends in the death of both the antagonists. And within Wacousta himself there is the conflict between the English gentleman he once was, before de Haldimar stole his bride from him, and the savage — more cruel than any Indian — whom he became in his search for revenge.

Less violent, but no less real in terms of shaping *Roughing It in the Bush*, is the conflict Susanna Moodie wages with the Yankee settlers and the Canadians who imitate them. They scorn and persecute her as an English lady, and she in turn scarifies in prose the crudity of their egalitarian behaviour with such disdain that it is a little surprising to be reminded that the Moodies, despite their rejection of Mackenzie and his rebellion, were radicals of their own kind and admirers of the reforming Baldwins. The rebellion appropriately ends the book; it is the conflict that releases the Moodies from their seven years of battle against the bush and their hostile neighbours.

The recurrence of personal conflict, interspersed with periods of suffering from the intractable forces of nature, gives *Roughing It in the Bush* its restless and episodic form, in comparison with *The Backwoods of Canada*, in which the tone of mild enthusiasm and the smoothly running narrative seem the very expressions of a persistent urge towards reconciliation. That urge is evident on a human level in the almost idyllic account of Traill's relations with the local Indians and on a natural level in the loving intimacy with which she observes the land, its beautiful flowers, its strange and intriguing fauna. It is evident, from the few disagreeable scenes which are recorded, that Traill endured many of the difficulties and the disappointments with neighbours that form the substance of her sister's book, but the difficulties are shown to be temporary and the personal disappointments exceptional, so that instead of ending, as *Roughing It* does, with a relieved escape from the slavery of the bush and a last chapter entitled "Adieu to the Woods," *The Backwoods of Canada* nears its close with Catharine Parr Traill telling her English correspondent that,

> . . . for all its roughness, I love Canada, and am as happy in my humble log-house as if it were courtly hall or bower; habit reconciles us to many things that at first were distasteful. It has ever been my way to extract the sweet rather than the bitter in the cup of life, and surely it is best and wisest so to do.[7]

In a similar way, Rosanna Leprohon seeks in *Antoinette de Mirecourt* to exemplify the process of reconciliation which she believed must be attained between the French in Canada and the English intruders. In some ways, her own life had been an exemplification of that reconciliation; the daughter of an Irish merchant settled in Montreal, she had married a well-known French-Canadian doctor and had turned from the fiction about another country (five serialized novels set in England) that she wrote before her marriage to the series of novels sympathetically regarding French-Canadian life, of which *Antoinette de Mirecourt* was the most successful. (The others were *Armand Durand; or, A Promise Fulfilled* and "The Manor House de Villeroi," which still awaits publication in volume form.)

The subtitle — "Secret Marrying and Secret Sorrowing" — sets the tone for one aspect of *Antoinette de Mirecourt*, a Victorian novel in which the author's frequent moralizing comments present the lesson that honour and honesty should govern relationships, not merely between the sexes, but between the generations. Antoinette is tricked into a secret marriage with a British officer, Major Audley Sternfield, and is then forced into a tortuous path of deception towards the world and towards her devoted father. Sternfield represents one face of the conquerors — the rapacious one; he married Antoinette because she is an heiress, but he combines greed (and need) with a desire to dominate and humiliate, and in drawing his character Leprohon seems to be portraying the kind of men who — whether they came as soldiers or commercially minded civilians with an eye to the main chance — treated the French as a subject people to be dominated and plundered.

Fortune releases Antoinette when Sternfield is killed in a duel, and then it is that a different conqueror appears, in the person of the grave and compassionate Colonel Evelyn, a man who sympathizes with, and seeks to understand, the French Canadians, and whose goodness converts Antoinette's father from his indiscriminate hatred of the foreigners. Not only is Antoinette rescued from the consequences of her youthful folly, but a reconciliation of the two peoples is prefigured in her marriage to the noble colonel. The contrast between the novel of conflict and the novel of reconciliation is curiously demonstrated by the fact that Colonel Evelyn, like Wacousta, is a man who has been scarred by a betrayal in love, but the experience that turned one man into a monster has turned the other into something near to a secular saint.

Thus, in many ways, through conflict and the reconciliation of conflict, we see the early Canadian writers in English presenting the ways in which the pioneers (including the conquerors) came to terms with their new world, not only as an unfamiliar and at first apparently hostile terrain which had to be brought under cultivation, but also as the habitation of earlier human societies which had to be controlled or conciliated in order to create a new English-speaking society. In the process, attitudes had to be changed. The pride of the conqueror had to be abandoned, as Colonel Evelyn abandoned his. The very class attitudes that sustained the structure of English society had to be shed, for, as Susanna Moodie shows near the end of *Roughing It in the Bush*, the needs of the new life had elevated the practical abilities of the working man over the social virtues of the gentleman:

> I have given you a faithful picture of a life in the backwoods of Canada, and I leave you to draw from it your own conclusions. To the poor, industrious working man it presents many advantages; to the poor gentleman, *none*! The former works hard, puts up with coarse, scanty fare, and submits, with a good grace, to hardships that would kill a domesticated animal at home. Thus he becomes independent, inasmuch as the land that he has cleared finds him in the common necessaries of life; but it seldom, if ever, in remote situations, accomplishes more than this. The gentleman can neither work so hard, live so coarsely, nor endure so many privations as his poorer but more fortunate neighbour. Unaccustomed to manual labour, his services in the field are not of a nature to secure for him a profitable return. The task is new to him, he knows not how to perform it well; and, conscious of his deficiency, he expends his little means in hiring labour, which his bush-farm can never repay. Difficulties increase, debts grow upon him, he struggles in vain to extricate himself, and finally sees his family sink into hopeless ruin.[8]

Yet, as Michael A. Peterman remarks, the enduring impressions one gains from *Roughing It* is that "the pattern of adaptation, of learning through experience, prevails,"[9] and indeed the Moodies did eventually find their place in Canadian society, and Susanna never went home.

It is perhaps accidental that the one among these early Canadian writers in whom the theme or pattern of reconciliation never makes a significant appearance should also be the first Canadian-born writer in English of any significance, John Richardson. Yet Richardson's birth in Upper Canada, his immersion from childhood in the lore of frontier warfare, and his actual participation as a boy in the War of 1812 seem to have precipitated what Dennis Duffy terms his "lifelong preoccupation with the terror of existence." Certainly the need for conflict was burnt into Richardson's nature, so that even the fleeting alliance between whites and Indians he had seen in the cooperation of Brock and Tecumseh, and celebrated in his appalling poem *Tecumseh; or, The Warrior of the West*, was superseded by the conflict, black with brutality and treachery, between the two races in *Wacousta*.

Richardson always remained a man at war with his world; *Wacousta* was projected from within. He existed in a milieu of self-created enmities and, unlike the Moodies and the Traills, never found a way of living in his own country, so that he spent years in England, fought in Spain during the Carlist wars, and became the first Canadian expatriate writer, dying in poverty in New York in 1852. Why were Richardson's fate and his writing so different from those of the other writers discussed in this essay? Was it because he remained at heart a child of the garrison and frontier warfare, locked in a world of fear that made him take so naturally to the Gothic manner and prevented him from finding a place in the changing world of the clearings and the towns?

As Richardson's choice of the Gothic suggests, there is a more than analogical link between the colonial life which was their subject matter and the search for appropriate forms that one sees among the writers discussed in this book. Like the pioneer farmers, the pioneer writers began by attempting to recreate the lost world of their childhood or their fathers in literary terms. But, again like the settlers, they found that the old approaches did not always fit the new circumstances.

It is true that one finds among the books of these writers examples of most of the genres that were fashionable in Britain at the time or sometimes at a slightly earlier date. There are Richardson's Gothicisms, which remind one of Monk Lewis and Maturin, as well as of Brockden Brown; there are the boys' adventure fictions of De Mille's B.O.W.C. series (reminiscent in more than title of the tales in the B.O.P. — *Boy's Own Paper*) and the quasi utopia of his *A*

Strange Manuscript Found in a Copper Cylinder; there are the romantic, yet moralistic, novels of Rosanna Leprohon and the awkward fiction of social conscience of Agnes Maule Machar; there are the Strickland sisters' narratives of imperial settlement, analogues of which can be found in other colonial literatures; and there is Frances Brooke's novel of sentiment, written in an epistolary form that was made famous by Samuel Richardson but which originated with women writers like Aphra Behn in the seventeenth century.

And yet, though all these authors follow patterns established in Britain, there are interesting ways in which their best works depart from Old World models, while their worst works — like Moodie's poems or Richardson's *Tecumseh* — are those in which they fail to realize that literature, like life, must adapt to a changed world. And thus, in a few key works of this early period of Canadian writing, one can see already the variations that in the end, to take up the metaphor with which I began this essay, acquire the distinctness and the endurance that make us recognize a new species. One cannot yet detach the works to which I have been referring from English literature, but one can certainly recognize in them English literature with a difference and at a distance.

We return to the Talmans' question in *Literary History of Canada* about *The History of Emily Montague*:

> Is it a novel only, or might it be classed also with description and travel literature?

It is a question that must be balanced by the tendency of some critics to consider the ostensibly factual accounts of pioneer experiences by writers like Moodie and Traill as being — or at least being comparable to — novels. Writing on Traill, Carl P.A. Ballstadt mentions the treatment by T.D. MacLulich of *The Backwoods* and *Roughing It* "as versions of the 'Crusoe' fable,"[10] and Michael A. Peterman notes how Carl F. Klinck argued of *Roughing It* that ". . . the book is best read as a novel that gains by 'concentration' upon Moodie's dramatization of herself as 'author-apprentice-heroine.'"[11]

What these critics are really suggesting is that in the pioneer period there was a blurring of the boundaries between the various literary genres. Much of the fiction of the time not only was very didactic but also tended to be heavily descriptive of the environment and at times to resemble contemporary travel writing. For example, the earlier part of *A Strange Manuscript Found in a Copper Cylinder*, which tells of Adam More's wanderings when he is first lost in the Antarctic, reads very much like a pastiche of nineteenth-century polar-exploration narratives.

But to say that sometimes fiction resembles travel writing — and perhaps vice versa — is not to surrender to the current North American academic snobbery which elevates the "creative" genres of fiction and poetry and seeks to find elements of the novel or the poem in works written with neither fictional nor lyrical intent. Travel writing and autobiography have their own ways of dealing with the palpable difference between the merely factual and the wholly true, and it is not necessary to declare an autobiographical memoir like *Roughing It in the Bush* a novel merely because Susanna Moodie shapes her narrative with artifice, rearranges episodes, and heightens the chiaroscuro of characterization to present a story that will catch the reader's attention. Every auto-biographer, every travel writer, even every historian or biographer with a pretension to being a good writer, does the same, and one might as justly call Donald Creighton's *The Empire of the St. Lawrence*, that splendid historical myth, a novel as apply the same description to *Roughing It in the Bush*. Both books are examples of the way in which the inchoate mass of facts — the crude data of experience — must be shaped by the writer to give it the feeling of truth. But that does not make them fiction in the sense we normally recognize, that of invention. And here, I think, we have to recognize a basic characteristic of emergent literatures: that they tend to be concerned with what William Godwin called "Things as They Are" and carry very little in the way of allegorical overload. Here I find particularly appropriate some sentences I have just read in a new essay on Homer:

> The allegorizing process tends to generalize every character or action into an abstraction. No poetry is less susceptible to this process than Homer's. . . . It has no hidden meanings. Every-thing described in it is intensely and uniquely itself.[12]

It is in this way, I suggest, that we must look at all beginning literatures. They are dealing with experiences that are new, but unassimilated into a new culture. They may use tried or traditional forms, in the same way as Homer used oral modes that had become formalized over centuries. Yet they are talking of the pristine and particular, not the accustomed and generalized. They are telling, like Homer, of something that, because it has not yet been subsumed into a settled order, is "intensely and uniquely itself." We do not have to look for layers of concealed meaning, partly because the writers with whom we are dealing are urgently concerned with what is there in pristine physical actuality or — in the case of the Richardsons — in dreadful imagined reality, but partly also because the culture itself has not yet developed the system of myths and symbols that will transform it from an almost accidental meeting of people and terrain into a distinctive cultural identity, a true species.

NOTES

[1] "Three Writers of Victorian Canada," in *Canadian Writers and Their Works*, ed. Robert Lecker, Jack David, and Ellen Quigley, Fiction ser. 1 (Downsview: ECW, 1983), p. 217; hereafter cited as *CWTW*.

[2] James J. Talman and Ruth Talman, "Settlement, Part III: The Canadas 1763–1812," in *Literary History of Canada: Canadian Literature in English*, gen. ed. and introd. Carl F. Klinck (Toronto: Univ. of Toronto Press, 1965), p. 85.

[3] Frances Brooke, *The History of Emily Montague* (1769; rpt. New York: Garland, 1974), 1, 216–17. All further references to this work appear in the text.

[4] "Frances Brooke (1724–1789)" in *CWTW*, Fiction ser., 1, p. 31.

[5] Catharine Parr Traill, *The Backwoods of Canada: Being Letters from the Wife of an Emigrant Officer, Illustrative of the Domestic Economy of British America* (London: Charles Knight, 1836), p. 123.

[6] *CWTW*, Fiction ser., 1, p. 111.

[7] Traill, *The Backwoods of Canada*, p. 310.

[8] Susanna Moodie, *Roughing It in the Bush; or, Life in Canada*, 2nd ed. (London: Bentley, 1852), II, 289–90.

[9] "Susanna Moodie (1803–1885)" in *CWTW*, Fiction ser., 1, p. 89.

[10] "Catharine Parr Traill (1802–1899)" in *CWTW*, Fiction ser., 1, p. 161.

[11] Carl F. Klinck, Introd., *Roughing It in the Bush; or, Forest Life in Canada*, by Susanna Moodie, New Canadian Library, No. 31 (Toronto: McClelland and Stewart, 1962), p. XIV.

[12] K.W. Gransden, "Homer and the Epic," in *The Legacy of Greece: A New Appraisal*, ed. M.I. Finley (London: Oxford Univ. Press, 1981), p. 80.

CHAPTER 2

Has-Beens or Lasting Names?:
Charles G.D. Roberts, Gilbert Parker, Ernest Thompson Seton, Thomas Chandler Haliburton, Thomas McCulloch

I BEGIN this essay with a confession which I am sure few even among teachers of Canadian literature will find surprising, since most of them would probably have to repeat it. I have read much less than half of the thirty-odd novels and romances which Gilbert Parker released upon an apparently eager world. I have read by no means all the many volumes of romance and animal fiction that Charles G.D. Roberts wrote, not even *Barbara Ladd*, which sold eighty thousand copies in its day yet has long gone unheeded by all but the most determined of scholars. I have read five of Ernest Thompson Seton's many volumes and consider that I have gained enough insight into a largely self-repeating author to last me a lifetime unless I find a special reason to read further. William Kirby, who produced very little, and Thomas Chandler Haliburton, who has a different kind of appeal from the four others, are the only writers among the five discussed in this volume whom I have read *in extenso*. And I know that I am not exceptional, even in my own area of literary scholarship. Indeed, unless one has a special reason to make a close study, I cannot think of any motive beyond literary masochism that would induce a modern reader to plough through all of Parker's facile and meretricious, though once highly popular, writings.

We are faced, it is clear, with the critical problem of the Grand Has-Beens. It is true that even in his own day, the more knowledgeable critics rarely took Gilbert Parker very seriously. The lack of substance and the lack of historical understanding in his romances of the past were pointed out even in his own day. But for a long time he was an extremely popular writer, in Britain and the United States as well as in Canada. Indeed, when I was an adolescent in England during the 1920s, the only Canadian writers whose names and works were at all familiar were Parker and two of the other writers here discussed, Roberts and Seton, with Archie Belaney in the Indian guise of Grey Owl sneaking up a little later. People were beginning to read Parker by then as they read current best sellers like Rafael Sabatini, as a shallow romancer, and even in comparison with the popular masters like Sir Walter Scott, Harrison Ainsworth, and Dumas père, Parker's *The Seas of the Mighty* seemed to me a flimsy work, a trivialization of history. I did, indeed, find much more to interest me in his *When Valmond Came to Pontiac* (though I was initially disappointed to discover that the title had misled me into believing that Valmond had paid a visit to the great Indian chief Pontiac), and I read two of the later "Pontiac" books, *The Pomp of the Lavilettes* and *The Lane That Had No Turning*, since the picture of Quebec life they gave me seemed quaint and intriguing. I accepted that picture as authentic, only to realize later that Parker's novels had the same kind of relationship to real Quebec life as Cornelius Krieghoff's paintings, the details vivid and often correct, but the real form of life in some way lacking. I was, admittedly, reading Parker in the last decade of his life, when his vogue was fast waning because World War I and its aftermath in revolution and economic crisis had destroyed the possibility of looking on the world with such gaudy simplicity as he offered. Even so, it seems to me particularly significant of the rapidity of Parker's decline that a young reader, who was only beginning to become acquainted with the early works of literary modernism, should already have reacted with a notable lack of the enthusiasm a previous and more politically innocent generation had shown towards Parker.

Perhaps the word *politically* is the most important in the previous sentence. For, on a somewhat less impressive level than Disraeli or Bulwer Lytton, Parker was a writer-politician in whom the two strands of his ambition seemed to be equally powerful. His novels, to be understood at any level higher than their lost entertainment value, have to be considered with this in mind. They embody attitudes towards imperialism, and towards the relationship between the French and English in Canada, that were highly fashionable on a political level in the English Canada of his time, and which made the British think of him as an authentic spokesman for Canada. Even in terms of style, the political element permeated Parker's novels. He had once been a teacher of elocution, and in the pursuit of politics, which took him to the British House of Commons and a baronetcy, he made use of the qualities that Gordon Roper, writing in the *Literary History of Canada: Canadian Literature in English*, found in his novels, particularly in those of the North West — a "strong melodramatic flair and elocutionary rhetoric."[1] Whatever else his novels may have lacked, the best of them, such as *When Valmond Came to Pontiac*, had considerable panache, and panache is a quality that flourishes best in a political context. Moreover, when he turned to his writing, Parker exemplified the fatal politician's inclination to substitute rhetoric if he was short on facts or feeling.

Yet the reasons for Parker's fall from the high days of his popularity, when, as Waterston remarks,[2] his novels presented visions of life "acceptable to hundreds of thousands," cannot be related to the politics to which he gave expression in his fiction. It is interesting at this point to compare his fate with that of his contemporary Sara Jeannette Duncan, whose work, as Waterston at one point remarks, "never rivalled Parker's in popularity." But interest in Duncan, whose works also went through a period of neglect after her death, is reviving with amazing rapidity, while interest in Parker remains stagnant and is likely to continue so. Yet both dealt with the politics of their time, and nothing is more out of tune with contemporary political attitudes than the Canadian debate over nationalism and imperialism exemplified in Duncan's *The Imperialist* or that over the policies of the Raj on the verge of decline embodied in her *The Burnt Offering*. The differences between Parker and Duncan are numerous, but those that seem most germane to their respective powers of survival lie in the fact that Duncan developed style while Parker developed rhetoric, that Duncan's characters, for all their wit and sparkle, were genuine, feeling human beings whereas Parker's were all too often romantic puppets, and that Duncan managed the detail of actuality with skill and imagination, so that her places always seemed real whereas Parker's places seem the projections of a quaint or sentimental fantasy, rather like those of the pseudo-historical musical comedy that flourished in his heyday.

As Waterston remarks, ". . . it would be a brave critic who would now see Parker as his contemporaries did, as an intellectual and splendidly gifted writer," and clearly a belief in his literary excellence was not the reason for his inclusion in this volume. Like other Grand Has-Beens, he remains interesting mainly because he was once popular, and because his popularity tells us something about the taste of his age, and this in turn about social values that have long been abandoned. From a critical point of view, Parker has to be dismissed as a writer ranging from mediocre to bad who offers little to interest us now. But as a figure in cultural history he remains of interest, and even of importance.

The same applies to the other writers under consideration, for all of them were oriented towards issues — political or social or philosophic — that were important in their times, and to whose discussion they owed a great deal of their popularity. None of these authors, in fact, would have written as he did if he had not been taken up with these issues — animal rights for Seton, Loyalist Toryism for Kirby, Nova Scotian revival for Haliburton. What perhaps unites them most is a tendency towards intellectual atavism. They look back, like Parker and Kirby and at times Roberts, to a human past that was more romantic than the mundane present; or, like Seton, and Roberts in his more successful fiction, to an animal world where good and evil are more clearly marked and destinies more sharply defined than in the human world; or, like Haliburton, to a comfortable Tory past when everybody knew his place and satire was the good Augustan device for the correction of manners. Rarely do any of these authors offer a realistic presentation of the human here-and-now.

William Kirby's name has often been associated with Parker's, because Parker is known to have admired the earlier author's single novel, *The Golden Dog*, and because the consensus of critics seems to be that Kirby's novel was a great deal better as historical fiction than *The Seats of the Mighty*, which appears to have been written in a spirit of emulation.

Kirby is a phenomenon with which we have become very familiar in Canada — the one-book writer. In fact, he wrote much more than the novel by which he is justly remembered, but part of his output went into the daily drudgery of small-town journalism and part into heavily didactic poetry that seems uninspired even in comparison with that of his contemporaries, such as Charles Sangster and Charles Heavysege. Like Heavysege, Kirby was a good example of that very English and very Victorian phenomenon, the self-taught Tory working man, and his self-acquired learning had the same kind of awesomely universal quality as the lightly borne erudition of Al Purdy in our own day.

Somehow, his passion for history and his besetting didacticism came together in *The Golden Dog* to produce what John Moss has well described as "a pot-boiler of high order, intended to sustain the reader's interest, remain true to the historical evidence, and deliver a message, all at the same time."[3] For a Canadian nineteenth-century novel, *The Golden Dog* has had an amazing record of success. When it appeared, it was widely acclaimed, and Kirby was sensibly content with his triumph; although he lived almost thirty years after its publication, he never made any attempt to repeat his success with a second historical novel. Unlike *The Seats of the Mighty*, *The Golden Dog* was not merely a best seller in its own time; it was that much rarer phenomenon, a best seller that retains its interest and its readership over generations. It was reprinted many times in the late nineteenth and early twentieth centuries, and even today it can be obtained — lamentably abridged — in the New Canadian Library series. When I returned to Canada in 1949, at a time when the literary landscape was far sparser than it is today, I heard *The Golden Dog* still being referred to as one of the major works of Canadian fiction.

The case against Kirby has perhaps been most strongly put by Margot Northey in her book *The Haunted Wilderness*, in which she seeks to sort out the true and the false Gothic strains in Canadian writing. From this point of view *The Golden Dog* is dismissed as irremediably ersatz.

Since the gothic elements in *The Golden Dog* do not effectively represent profound inner anxieties or fears, they are merely melodramatic colouring. The reader can respond to this tale of thrills and chills with a certain detachment; he is sometimes apt to smile rather than to take it seriously.

·   ·   ·   ·   ·   ·   ·   ·   ·   ·   ·   ·

The Golden Dog, despite its obvious attention to details of history and geography, presents life with a drop of faked bitters and a spoonful of sugar. Despite its overlay of conventional images of horror, Kirby's romance does not confront the problematic or ambiguous in life, but rather it supplies a comfortable cushion from which one can vicariously enjoy the exotic adventures of another time while resting secure and assured. Like so many lesser works which preceded and followed it, the gothicism in *The Golden Dog* is decorative rather than truly functional.[4]

Not surprisingly, Northey reveals that she prefers John Richardson's *Wacousta*.

But were Kirby's intentions really Gothic? Is it not the fact that his Gothic decorations are so obviously veneer a reason to seek some rather different aim in his novel and, given that possibility, some different kind of achievement? What if, given Kirby's close interest in history and his Tory politics, he was seeking ultimately to portray a reality quite different from the Gothic fantasy into which he sometimes slips by Victorian habit, and to teach a very down-to-earth historical lesson? Many critics have noticed how much more solidly based his work is in historical fact than Parker's melodramatic treatments of the past, and Moss shows very clearly, I think, the way in which Kirby uses his mastery of historical fact to preach a political lesson, a lesson which, since it depends on the maintenance of the postconquest relationship between English and French in Canada, we must now regard as reactionary, in the strict backward-turning sense of that greatly misused word.

Kirby's fiction is so well wedded to historical conditions that the impending fall of Quebec seems an inevitable consequence of the moral turbulence Kirby portrays. That is part of Kirby's message: the fall was inevitable. And, by historical implication, the British presence was a moral necessity. (Moss, p. 142)

Read in the context of modern Canadian fiction, read even in comparison with such sophisticated nineteenth-century writers as James De Mille and Sara Jeannette Duncan, *The Golden Dog* often seems an awkward, if — despite its superficial artificialities — an honest, book. And perhaps the awkwardness has something to do with the honesty, which is not necessarily an aid to good writing. I think the best brief summary of these aspects of Kirby is that given by W.J. Keith in his *Canadian Literature in English*:

> The events of the story are filtered through Kirby's stiff but consistently dignified style, and even when the willing sus-pension of disbelief is hardest, narrative interest is maintained. The principal characters may seem too good (or bad) to be true, but they nevertheless achieve a human individuality. For all its faults (especially conspicuous if we persist in invoking the hardly relevant criteria of realistic fiction), this is perhaps the most substantial narrative written in Canada in the nine-teenth century.[5]

Substantial yes, but hardly subtle; though, as Keith indicates at another point:

> A curious tension is produced between the exaggerated emo-tions and romantic actions on the one hand, and the lovingly minute and factually exact descriptions of houses, public buildings, feasts, and local customs on the other. (Keith, p. 44)

Readers of the volume of *Canadian Writers and Their Works* could not fail to be impressed by the extent to which Terry Whalen's study of Charles G.D. Roberts was about Ernest Thompson Seton and Lorraine McMullen's study of Ernest Thompson Seton was about Charles G.D. Roberts. This is doubtless inevitable because of what at first sight seems the astonishing synchronicity of their involvement in the creation of the animal story, which, in the form they developed, is — as we have so often been told by Margaret Atwood and less conspicuous authorities — Canada's special contribution to the fiction of the English-speaking world. Since both Whalen and McMullen devote attention to the still-debated question of who was the real originator in this case, it seems hardly necessary to continue the argument, except perhaps to note the resemblance between this controversy and the classic and peren-nially reopened argument over who first conceived the idea of evolution by natural selection, Charles Darwin or Alfred Russel

Wallace. That controversy has been going on for generations, with its periodic outbursts of accusation and recrimination, when the simplest solution seems to lie in accepting Kropotkin's suggestion that certain ideas naturally develop, before they are expressed, from the intellectual circumstances of an age and float free, as it were, waiting for someone to articulate them. In such circumstances it is not surprising that two or more inquirers should hit upon the same idea more or less simultaneously, and in fact the history of science is studded with such synchronicities.

The need to prove whether Seton or Roberts was foremost in inventing the animal story seems even less urgent if we accept Atwood's thesis that the Canadian type of animal story, which the two of them were undoubtedly the first to write, owed its existence, if not to a peculiar formation of the Canadian psyche, at least to a peculiar view Canadians have of their fate in the modern world. Proceeding from Desmond Morris' studies of how various age-groups of people tend to identify with particular types of animals, Atwood sees a special Canadian identification with wild animals, suggesting the likelihood that

> . . . Canadians themselves feel threatened and nearly extinct as a nation, and suffer also from life-denying experience as individuals — the culture threatens the "animal" within them — and that their identification with animals is the expression of a deep-seated cultural fear. The animals, as Seton says, are us. And for the Canadian animal, bare survival is the main aim in life, failure as an individual is inevitable, and extinction as a species is a distinct possibility.[6]

While I do not accept in their entirety Atwood's arguments about the overriding thematic importance of survival as a basis for interpreting Canadian literature, there is no doubt that she and James Polk have variously been correct in pointing out that English Canadian animal stories, as represented in the work of Roberts and Seton and of their successors like Farley Mowat and Fred Bodsworth, are strikingly different from the bulk of British or American or even French Canadian animal stories. The English Canadians never developed the kind of tradition of folk fable that the ancestors of the Québécois brought with them from France, and, though Susanna Moodie and some of her contemporaries seem to have experimented with the English type of story in which the animals are really fur-clad human beings, the daily experience of contact with animals and of observing their ways prevented such a convention from taking hold among Canadians; at the same time, it must be pointed out that here the Atwood-Polk case is not watertight, since some British writers like Henry Williamson wrote animal biographies not unlike those of Seton.

The difference between the American and the Canadian animal story is perhaps more interesting, because both are based on experience in the wilderness, and in both the animal tends to appear as the quarry and the human as the hunter. The difference is that in all of Seton's stories and in almost all of Roberts' (there are exceptions, such as *The Heart of the Ancient Wood*) the reader's sympathies are recruited for the animal in its endeavour to outwit its pursuer and survive until the next encounter, while in the case of American animal stories sympathy is generally evoked for the hunter, for whom the animal often provides the challenge that must be met as a rite of passage. Here again, however, the distinction is not entirely clear-cut, since the stories of both Seton and Roberts were popular in the United States as well as Canada, and some American writers, like Jack London, do come near in attitude to their Canadian counterparts.

But granting that Canadian animal stories are sympathetic to animals, with whom their readers are induced to identify, this does not mean that the relations between humans and animals are seen in terms of a shared threat of extinction, a shared inevitability of failure, as Atwood seems to suggest. As both Whalen and McMullen repeatedly point out, the animals in the best stories of Seton and Roberts are presented as heroes; indeed, they are among the few real heroes in Canadian literature. They are usually portrayed as "fine specimens," leaders of their kind in terms of both strength and intelligence, and, especially in Seton's "biographies," they repeatedly evade and frustrate their human antagonists; some even terrorize whole countrysides for long periods before they eventually meet death, which is the fate of us all, humans and animals alike. Sometimes, even, nature takes its revenge on the killer of the animal hero, who in this way is ultimately vindicated.

If all this is to be related in any way with the attitudes of human

Canadians, I would suggest it betokens an attitude of defiance and fortitude, in which survival — if that is the thought in mind — becomes a matter of triumph rather than of minimal achievement. But I still wonder whether in both Seton and Roberts it was not a matter of scientific fashion rather than an expression of national identity. For it would be hard to find better fictional exemplifications than their earlier animal stories of the Huxleyan adaptation of Darwin's doctrine, with its strong emphasis on the struggle for existence, as distinct from Kropotkin's alternative emphasis on mutual aid as a dominant factor in evolution. This is not to say that the influence of *Mutual Aid: A Factor of Evolution* was entirely lacking after that book's appearance in 1902. It is certainly suggested in Seton's later animal biographies, where the role of the leader animal in knitting the herd or pack together for mutual protection and advantage is stressed; it is also suggested in the inclination of both Roberts and Seton to stress the idea of the kinship between humans and animals that acceptance of evolutionary theory makes possible.

There are obvious differences, as both McMullen and Whalen recognize, between the attitudes of Seton and Roberts towards their material, though both of them, since they wrote so often of animal lives that are very much alike in their progression through a series of escapes towards the final, unavoidable scene of death, tended to create patterns that became monotonous in their repetition, so that, as Whalen remarks, ". . . Roberts reads much better in selection than he does in dutiful bulk."

Throughout his career Seton was, in intent at least, the scientist foremost, and in some ways, such as his stress on the need to maintain ecological balances and to save threatened species, he was a remarkably farsighted one for his day. Indeed, what McMullen really fails to observe in her essay is the extent to which, as a writer, Seton stands within the nineteenth-century scientific tradition and somewhat outside the literary tradition.

Yet the particular branch of the scientific tradition to which he adhered was then, in its own way, committed to literary values. Its sources can be found in the practices of The Royal Society of London for Improving of Natural Knowledge, founded in the late seventeenth century. The society brought writers like Dryden together with the entirely amateur scientists of the day, like Prince

HAS-BEENS OR LASTING NAMES?

Rupert and Robert Boyle, at a time when the requirements of the developing natural sciences called for a precision of prose statement that had not before existed; clear expository English prose dated from the recognition of that need. The times when scientists would create their own obfuscatory jargons were far ahead, and among the naturalists especially a tradition of good writing was established, exemplified in the eighteenth-century observation records of Gilbert White of Selborne and carried on in the writings of the nineteenth-century naturalists. The great evolutionist pioneers, Darwin and Wallace, T.H. Huxley and Henry Walter Bates, all went on long journeys of observation and collection before they returned to distil their findings into scientific treatises, and the muse of Dryden and the Royal Society hovered over them when they wrote the marvellous narratives of their travels — notably Darwin's *The Voyage of the Beagle* and Bates's *The Naturalist on the Amazons* — in evocative and limpid prose. But none of the early naturalists recognized the possibilities of fiction as a way to catch their readers' attention and implant their lessons more deeply. Even W.H. Hudson, who wrote some excellent fiction at the same time as he was writing his classic volumes on Argentinean and British birds, never actually wrote stories in which animals appeared as fictional characters. Seton was the first man of scientific bent to recognize the possibilities of fiction as a way of presenting his knowledge of the natural world, and so when he came to writing his stories, it was less as a man of letters than as a man of science. As Alec Lucas remarks in the *Literary History of Canada*:

> As a writer-naturalist, Seton is much less interested in the art of fiction than in telling a true tale (although "Krag" is a fine short story) and imparting knowledge of the outdoors. His usual method is to stress narrative and events. Yet he does tell good stories, for he never lets his natural history override his narrative, and his events are interesting in themselves. Moreover his success depends, too, on the way in which he appeals to his reader for sympathy with the animal world.[7]

The problem of how far Seton's stories can really be accepted as fiction has troubled many critics. Keith sees them as existing "in a no man's land between fiction and non-fiction; his fiction invariably has a non-fiction purpose in that it is representative, illustrative of events continually taking place in the "wilderness" (Keith, p. 46). But other critics have been impressed by the literary virtues of Seton's writings; Clara Thomas says that "his stories are finely written, full of colour and detail and always deepened by [his] sense of death and tragic waste."[8] And her observations are just.

It seems to me that Seton became a good writer almost by default. Having decided that stories gave a more vivid presentation of what he had observed of life in the wild than narrative essays, he was taken up in the process of creation and wrought better than he knew, or at least than he expected, which is why many of his stories are still so readable. His choice of form also accounts for why literal-minded outdoorsmen, including Theodore Roosevelt speaking *ex cathedra* from the White House, found it necessary to attack him for alleged anthropomorphism, and in this way forced him into the kind of self-defence, like that quoted by McMullen, in which he opts, if the choice must be made, for art over science:

> The subject of my first book, and indeed of all my books, was the *personality* of the individual animal. No man can write of another personality without adding a suggestion of his own. The personal touch may be the poison of science, but may also be the making of literature, and is *absolutely inevitable*.[9]

Yet he continued to maintain that his stories were true to life and therefore, in all that counted, scientifically respectable.

> Finally I maintain that my stories do convey a true notion of the ways of the animals, their troubles, their trials, their matings, their friendships, and their foes; the lives they live and the deaths they die.[10]

In fact, he did endow his animals with powers of intelligence and reasoning which cannot be proved scientifically, though they may in fact exist, and in this sense he was relying on the powers of imagination rather than those of observation, and creating true if uneven fiction.

In Canadian literary history, Charles G.D. Roberts probably looms largest as a poet, though lately his once ascendant repute has been lessening in comparison with those of Archibald Lampman and Duncan Campbell Scott. Now Terry Whalen makes the claim that "while [Roberts'] poetry ostensibly leads us onto firmer ground because of its mythic certainties, his fiction speaks more directly to writing in our own day." Whalen bases this assertion on his opinion that ". . . an intimate, almost transparent connection between diction and object, between the word and the experienced world, is the hallmark of Roberts' best writing."

The trouble with such an argument is that Roberts is all too often not at his best, and that, especially in his early romances, he produced a vast amount of fuzzy and unfocused writing that speaks to nothing but the passing modes of the time when it was written. Even in that ambitious and supremely well-intentioned novel of the wild, *The Heart of the Ancient Wood,* in which he attempted to establish a meaningful bond between human beings and the wilderness, he failed because he created a sentimental relationship of humans within untamed nature rather than an organic link, which is presumably what his idea of the kinship of animals and humans would have led him to aim at. What he achieved in that mawkish novel reminds one all too uncomfortably of the sentimental naturalist fiction of writers like Gene Stratton Porter.

It was when Roberts kept his human characters in the hostile role of the hunter that his stories were best, for then he could concentrate on the animal as an intelligent being with a will to survive, coping with the perils of a wild existence aggravated by human intervention, and could develop the themes which Lucas in the *Literary History of Canada* has defined as "the amorality of nature, the struggle for survival, [and] the cyclical aspect of time" (Lucas, p. 401)

Whalen tells us that "Roberts sees the realistic animal story — 'a psychological romance constructed on a framework of natural science' — as a genre which might promote a return to witness of, respect for, and wonder at the natural world." And this kind of moral purpose is indeed one element of Roberts' interest in the animal story. Another, and perhaps more important factor, was that kind of opportunism inevitable in the profession of man of letters, a tendency to use versatile talents where they will be most profitable, not merely in the sense of earning money but also in the sense of making the best artistic use of them. For there is no doubt that, while Roberts found the animal story a well-selling line of writing, he also found in it the form in which he shone best as a prose writer.

While Roberts thus seems to have shared to a great extent in Seton's moral purpose, wishing to induce people to accept their responsibility towards their animal kindred, he did not share Seton's scientific purpose. Lucas may be unnecessarily severe when he says that Roberts was "not a naturalist but a casual observer" (Lucas, p. 400); I suspect that Roberts did in fact have enough knowledge to qualify as an amateur naturalist by the standards of his time. Yet it remains true that, as Lucas adds,

> Despite his realism, [Roberts] did not write his "true" stories like Seton out of his experiences but, in large part, from hearsay and his reading. Consequently, his two hundred or so stories on almost every living creature are often inaccurate and lack something of the attractive intimacy of Seton's. (Lucas, p. 400)

Seton, too, as his critics often complained, was sometimes less than accurate in the way he would describe an animal's actions so as to make them more likely to arouse human sympathies, yet it is true that his close knowledge did give a feeling of greater intimacy to his stories; at the same time, Roberts' relative ignorance allowed him to be bolder in developing strong plots and striking situations. The animal story gave to both authors a distinctive and innovative role in Canadian writing.

Thomas Chandler Haliburton resembled Seton and Roberts in being innovative and well known, but in very little else. It is hard to think of anything more remote from their animal stories or from the romances of Parker and Kirby than the satirical writing, directed very closely at contemporary human societies, of *The Clockmaker* or *The Old Judge*; the most they share is a nostalgia for something different from the present. Neither the historical romances nor the animal stories are conceivable in a world that had not experienced the Romantic movement, but Haliburton wrote as if the Romantics had never existed, and it is appropriate that one of his many admirers in Britain should have been that other belated Augustan, Walter Savage Landor, who in 1858 addressed a poem to Haliburton:

Once I would bid the man go hang,
From whom there came a word of slang;
Now pray I, tho' the slang rains thick
Across the Atlantic from *Sam Slick*,
Never may fall the slightest hurt on,
The witty head of Haliburton,
Wherein methinks more wisdom lies
Than in the wisest of our wise.[11]

On the other hand, the American iconoclast and muckraker H.L. Mencken gave Haliburton a high rank among the originators of a really indigenous humour, by which he seems to have meant an indigenous *American* humour, for Haliburton, like Stephen Leacock, tended to be accepted as one of their own south of the border, despite the glaring Yankee defects of his creation Sam Slick.

And, indeed, it is with some diffidence that one talks of Haliburton as a Canadian writer, for, as Northrop Frye had remarked, "Haliburton would never have called himself a Canadian. He was a Nova Scotian, a Bluenose, and died two years before Confederation."[12] Haliburton had none of Joseph Howe's bounding visions of railways uniting the Maritime provinces with Canada and sending their locomotives echoing through the Rockies. With his links with Britain and his understanding of the American mind, Haliburton might perhaps be described as having an Atlantic Triangular world view, but his immediate political concerns were directed to Nova Scotia and did not foresee a Canadian connection.

Haliburton cannot be understood outside his politics, and his politics were essentially reactionary. As Stanley E. McMullin remarks, "His conservatism was anachronistic as an active political force very early in his career."[13] Haliburton seems to have believed quite sincerely that a functioning aristocratic society had once existed in which the class structure had actually guaranteed the freedom of everyone; as Moss remarks, he wanted "to reform society by returning to an ideal that never existed" (Moss, p. 115). Though he was not himself of Loyalist descent, Haliburton shared the Loyalist distrust of the American political system, and he refused to see in the responsible government sought by his friend Joseph Howe a means by which local desires for self-rule could be fulfilled without a drastic break with Britain. To the end,

Haliburton remained an unrepentant and unyielding colonialist.

But reactionary attitudes often attract good writers, and this seems to be even more the case with satire, where a Tory stance seems an excellent one from which to direct an attack on existing society. Moreover, reactionary political attitudes do not rule out progressive attitudes in fields such as agriculture, industry, even social welfare. The contradiction in classic Tories, of whom Haliburton was typical, is often that they envisage taking a political step back in order to take a social or an economic step forward.

Sam Slick was a triumph in satirical character creation because he enabled Haliburton to fulfil both his aims. In his cockiness and cunning and sharp dealing, Sam represented the worst side of the American character as Haliburton saw it, and suggested how public morals would decline under a republican government. On the other hand, Sam's criticisms of the sluggish ways of Nova Scotians in managing their social and economic affairs were sharp and pointed and meant to be taken seriously. If this obnoxious Yankee is able to despise us, Haliburton suggests, it is time we improved ourselves.

A great deal of the wordplay in *The Clockmaker* and the other "Sam Slick" books no longer seems very amusing, but Sam Slick is still preserved from tediousness by the sharpness of his aphoristic remarks on human behaviour, public and private. Frye perceptively remarks that

> Sam Slick is at his best when he's describing the country and its customs, and he's at his best often enough to bring Nova Scotia in the 1830s really to life. That doesn't make *The Clockmaker* provincial or antiquated; it makes it concrete.[14]

Haliburton began as a social historian with his *General Description of Nova Scotia* in 1823, and while his fiction is genuine enough in the sense that he creates convincing characters without giving their interconnections the psychological complexity that would justify our calling anything he wrote a novel, he remains to the end as much a storyteller with a sociopolitical aim as Seton was a storyteller with a scientific aim.

The end, so far as Haliburton's effective literary career is concerned, was of course *The Old Judge*, and as McMullin remarks, it is unfortunate that ". . . Sam Slick's international reputation overshadowed *The Old Judge* to such a degree that no Canadian edition of the book appeared until 1968 . . ."; even then it was an abridged edition. *The Old Judge* has its strong advocates. Moss declares it "far and away the best book Haliburton wrote" (Moss, p. 114), and other critics in recent years have noted its special virtues. Keith, for instance, remarks that it is "one of the first works in Canadian literature to look back in nostalgia to an earlier period in the country's development" (Keith, p. 18). And, indeed, with Sam's cleverness and Haliburton's expectations burnt away, there are characteristics of *The Old Judge*, a reflective power and a reminiscent honesty, that perhaps justify regarding it as the pioneer work of Canadian realistic fiction.

But not of Canadian satiric fiction, for that honour must go to Thomas McCulloch's *Letters of Mephibosheth Stepsure*, which were published serially in the *Acadian Recorder* between 1821 and 1823 and eventually as a volume in 1862. They were really sketches rather than stories, written by a pietistic social climber who reports on the misfortunes of the goats in his community, though the pious sheep who follow the admonitions of Dr. Drone do not escape his scorn and envy. The people who appear in the *Letters* are types rather than characters, but even before Haliburton, McCulloch shows a flair for realistic description — usually of the seedy and disreputable — and the succession through Haliburton to Leacock is evident. The borrowing of Dr. Drone is not the only clue to the succession. One can agree with Northrop Frye who said once that McCulloch was "the founder of Canadian humour; that is, of the humour which is based on a vision of society and is not merely a series of wisecracks on a single theme."[15] McCulloch was a lesser writer, and undoubtedly more important in his time as a divine and an educator, yet it is the writing that has lived and had its enduring influence, and *The Stepsure Letters* (as they have been called since their publication in the New Canadian Library in 1960) have shown themselves, as one says of apples, to be good keepers.

NOTES

1 Gordon Roper, S. Ross Beharriell, and Rupert Schieder, "Writers of Fiction, 1880–1920," in *Literary History of Canada: Canadian Literature in English*, 2nd ed., gen. ed. and introd. Carl F. Klinck (Toronto: Univ. of Toronto Press, 1976), 1, 331.

[2] Elizabeth Waterston, "Gilbert Parker and His Works," *Canadian Writers and Their Works*, ed. Robert Lecker, Jack David, and Ellen Quigley, Fiction ser., II (Toronto: ECW, 1989), p. 123; hereafter cited as *CWTW*.

[3] John Moss, *A Reader's Guide to the Canadian Novel* (Toronto: McClelland and Stewart, 1981), p. 141. All further references to this work (Moss) appear in the text.

[4] Margot Northey, *The Haunted Wilderness: The Gothic and Grotesque in Canadian Fiction* (Toronto: Univ. of Toronto Press, 1976), pp. 31–32.

[5] W.J. Keith, *Canadian Literature in English* (London: Longman, 1985), p. 44. All further references to this work (Keith) appear in the text.

[6] Margaret Atwood, *Survival: A Thematic Guide to Canadian Literature* (Toronto: House of Anansi, 1972), p. 79.

[7] Alec Lucas, "Nature Writers and the Animal Story," in Klinck, ed., *Literary History of Canada*, I, 398–99. All further references to this work (Lucas) appear in the text.

[8] Clara Thomas, *Our Nature — Our Voices: A Guidebook to English-Canadian Literature* (Toronto: new, 1972), p. 49.

[9] Ernest Thompson Seton, quoted in Julia Moss Seton, *By a Thousand Fires: Nature Notes and Extracts from the Life and Unpublished Journals of Ernest Thompson Seton* (Garden City, N.Y.: Doubleday, 1967), p. 73.

[10] Seton, p. 73.

[11] "To Judge Haliburton," rpt. in *Colombo's Canadian Quotations*, ed. John Robert Colombo (Edmonton: Hurtig, 1974), p. 322.

[12] Northrop Frye, "Haliburton: Mask and Ego," in *Beginnings*, Vol. II of *The Canadian Novel*, ed. John Moss (Toronto: NC, 1980), p. 40.

[13] "Thomas Chandler Haliburton and His Works," in *CWTW*, Fiction ser., II, p. 43.

[14] Frye, p. 43.

[15] Cited by Douglas Lochhead in *Oxford Companion to Canadian Literature*, ed. William Toye (Toronto: Oxford Univ. Press, 1983), p. 481.

CHAPTER 3

Madly Off in All Directions:
Stephen Leacock,
Sara Jeannette Duncan,
Ralph Connor, Robert Stead

CANADIAN LITERATURE is essentially centrifugal, tending incorrigibly towards regional, rather than national, orientations, and never so vital as when it is most varied, riding, like Stephen Leacock's Lord Ronald, "madly off in all directions." That is why it is salutary to encounter four writers from the same period who are so dissimilar in their work and in their attitude to writing, as those who are here discussed: Sara Jeannette Duncan and Charles W. Gordon (pseud. Ralph Connor), Stephen Leacock and Robert Stead. The very pairing of them off in this way points up their differences: for what can one imagine, more than a few commonplaces, would worldly-wise Duncan and muscular-Christian Gordon have had to say to each other, or for that matter, staid Stead and laughing Leacock?

What the four authors do join in teaching is that the same set of national circumstances can produce, as a literature becomes progressively more articulate, a surprising range of expressions. A nation, as it grows self-conscious, does not speak — as politically naïve nationalists like to believe — in a single voice; it speaks in many voices, and the more they differ from each other, the better.

The one thing that Stead and Duncan, Gordon and Leacock, have in common is that each of them, in his or her own way, gives authentic expression to an expansive Canada that had passed beyond the travails of Confederation: the Canada of the 1890s and the Edwardian era — Laurier's Canada rather than Macdonald's.

With the exception of Stead's *Grain*, which came out in 1926, all their important books were written and published during that period, and even *Grain* drew its inspiration from a view of the West that developed in the Laurier age. Every one of them was conscious of being present at a kind of national rendezvous with destiny, and one of the most interesting things about them is that they found so many ways of witnessing, from romance to realism, from the comedy of manners to the fictional tract, from erudite nonsense to evangelical earnestness.

Gordon and Stead derived from, and continued to write in, popular traditions, while Duncan and Leacock were in very different ways sophisticates — wits in the older English sense of the word — whom it is difficult to imagine outside the urban culture that was spreading in Canada at this time, a culture which had more links with the new city civilization of the eastern United States than with the traditional civilization of Europe. Duncan became the kind of writer she was by immersing herself in the new ways of journalism and of fiction writing that were being developed south of the border, and though she paid great tribute to George Eliot as a predecessor, there is no doubt that her real masters, insofar as she had any, were William Dean Howells and Henry James, and Howells more than James. Leacock also, despite his pronounced Anglophilia, belonged, insofar as he inhabited any tradition, in that of the North American humorists of whom Mark Twain, to whom he devoted an affectionate book, was the dean. Much as he admired Dickens, there is not a great deal in common between his concise and intellectually controlled sketches and the sprawling extravagances of the English writer.

Indeed, all of these writers, with the partial exception of Stead, wrote in an international context and depended on international audiences to a far greater extent than most Canadian writers today. In part this was because the national audience was smaller than it now is, though even then both Gordon and Leacock found hundreds of thousands of Canadian readers; but it was also because they wrote in a way that, even when they were writing about Canada, appealed to readers outside the country. Most of the five million copies that made Gordon's three most successful novels such phenomenal best sellers for their period were bought by readers in the United States and Britain, and the same applies to

Leacock's most popular works. Certainly in Britain at this period, "Ralph Connor" and Leacock were the only widely known Canadian authors, and even during World War II, when paper was so scarce that many English writers found it hard to gain publication, *Sunshine Sketches of a Little Town* was reprinted there in a large Penguin edition.

Sara Jeannette Duncan was in every way the most cosmopolitan of these writers, as Robert Stead was the least so. She spent the last half of her life abroad, in India and Britain, setting her novels in these countries as well as in Canada, and the editions of her books that appeared in London and New York undoubtedly sold better than those that appeared in Toronto. Yet, whenever her physical body might wander, Duncan never cut her mental ties with Canada, which she often revisited, and her sole novel set only in that country — *The Imperialist* — is not only one of her three best novels (her Indian books *His Honour, and a Lady* and *The Burnt Offering* being its rivals), but also offers an amazingly faithful recollective vision, particularly considering that it was written in India many years after Duncan left home.

The Imperialist presents most boldly a theme that is one way or another concerns all the four writers in this volume: Canada's emergence as a nation and, by corollary, its place in the international spectrum. And here it is significant of their sensitivity to the issues of their time that none of the four turned towards the United States as offering any future for Canada. Duncan may have worked for Goldwin Smith on *The Week* and may have admired contemporary American novelists more than she did their English counterparts, and Leacock may have been influenced by the American humorists and have set his *Arcadian Adventures with the Idle Rich* in some unspecified American city, but when it came to seeing a destiny for Canada, both of them came very near to that peculiar mingling of nationalism with imperialism that developed through the Canada First movement in earlier decades of the nineteenth century.

At the same time, Gordon's and Stead's novels show that they were both in no doubt of Canada's future being embodied in a western rather than a southern drive. While Duncan and Leacock were preoccupied with the idea of an empire where cooperation and equality — at least between its Anglo-Saxon inhabitants — would provide the keynote, the two Prairie writers were anticipating the idea of a pattern of development along the routes already established by the fur traders, from eastern Canada to the prairies and beyond, that would later become the subject of Donald Creighton's nationalist vision in *The Empire of the St. Lawrence* (1956). In this way, as happens so often, the insights of literary artists preceded those of the historians.

All this involved a loyalty to the British connection that would diminish in later generations of Canadian novelists, and at times there was a fervour about it that rose to hysterical levels when it became confused with religious emotion, as happened in one of Gordon's worst books, *The Sky Pilot in No Man's Land*, where patriotism takes on a kind of sadistic indecency as the chaplain Barry Dunbar, preaching to a battalion of soldiers on the Western Front, tells them of their duty to keep their bodies clean and fit so that they may be a proper sacrifice to God.

The British orientation also involved difficulties over the fact that Canada, and the Empire in general, contained other people than Anglo-Celts. Leacock avoided this problem by writing as if Canada were inhabited only by the English and the Scots. It is astonishing that a man so intelligent should have fitted so well into the stereotype of the blinkered Montreal Anglo by virtually ignoring the French-speaking majority in the city where he lived. In his own way, Stead also shared Leacock's disinclination to dwell on the possible problems of a multicultural nation and wrote of the Prairies as if the settling of them was mainly an Anglo-Saxon affair.

Both Duncan and Gordon did, in their own ways, confront the question. In India, Duncan was too sensitive, too independent-minded, and too much interested in the unfamiliar life around her to be able to behave, like the classic memsahib, as if the only Indians were the servants with whom she came into unavoidable contact. In common with the best of the sahibs, she saw the role of the British as the bringing of political maturity to India, so that she was never a critic of the Raj per se, even in the mild way of her acquaintance E.M. Forster. Yet in *His Honour, and a Lady*, she makes quite clear her preference for the hard-working, conscientious, and even dull official John Church, who sacrifices himself in the hope of bettering the lot of Indians, over the self-seeking careerist Lewis Ancram, who is concerned merely with rising through the ranks of the Indian Civil Service to the top, and who intrigues ruthlessly even against his supposed friends in order to succeed.

Duncan looked ironically on Anglo-Indian society, observing, in a manner that sometimes strikingly anticipated George Orwell's insight into the enslavement of the ruler by the ruled in "Shooting an Elephant," the way most of the sahibs were conditioned and diminished as persons by their narrow roles in the paranoiac Anglo-Indian world. At the same time, she showed a growing understanding of Indians and a growing sympathy for their involvement in the dilemma that imperial rule created for them as much as for their rulers. *The Burnt Offering*, written with much political understanding at a time when — just before the advent of Gandhi — the independence movement had taken on a violent aspect, is remarkable for the variety of its Indian cast, whose members show a wide range of approaches towards the question of gaining freedom from British rule, going all the way from noncooperation to terrorism. She is not merely aware of how Indians are thinking; by showing how they react in certain extreme situations, she also reveals an understanding of the Indian psychology that could only have come from the kind of careful observation of the "natives" any ordinary memsahib would have shunned with horror.

Similarly, considering how imperial and conservative his attitude could be in other ways, Gordon confronted with surprising insight the difficulties encountered by non-British immigrants in Canada. His novel *The Foreigner* was the rough fictional equivalent to J.S. Woodsworth's contemporary *Strangers within Our Gates; or, Coming Canadians* (1909) in its presentation of the predicament of people arriving without money in a strange land, neither of whose languages they speak. *The Foreigner* forms a natural bridge to the later years when Gordon — in his other persona as the Reverend Charles William Gordon — showed his sympathy for the working people of the West in their struggle for better conditions, notably in the Winnipeg General Strike, and became a preacher of the Social Gospel, even writing one novel about class conflict, *To Him That Hath*, which halts well on the safe side of militancy.

At the same time, Gordon seems to have remained content to note the presence of the French in Canada without feeling that discord is latent in the relations between them and the Anglo-Celts who mostly people his novels. As Roy Daniells suggested, he seems to have felt that the all-embracing nature of his imperial vision was enough:

> To the latent issues of French-speaking versus English-speaking cultures and of Catholic versus Protestant [Gordon] turns an unseeing eye. Readers of *The Man from Glengarry* may make what they will of the opening scene where the Irish-French gang is blocking the mouth of the river but gives way to the demands of the Glengarry gang for free passage of their logs. They can, if they wish, read significance into LeNoir, the French-Canadians' leader, who moves from murderous hostility to outright co-operation with Macdonald. [Gordon's] own emphasis is on western expansion as absorptive of all energies, a cure for all enmities. The imperial theme of the dominion fills his imagination, transcendence enters as his solution, and "Glengarry forever!" becomes more than a cry to rally a clan: it is the talisman, all suggestive and all sufficient, of [Gordon's] sense of greatness.[1]

Having observed that our four writers shared, and were conscious of sharing, an expansive time in Canadian history and, in political and social terms, reacted in similar ways since all of them saw the westward drive beyond the original two Canadas through imperially tinted lenses, one must now observe how different they were in the ways they wrote about what they perceived, and indeed in their attitudes towards the very art of writing.

In my view, Sara Jeannette Duncan stands quite apart from the rest, both as a professional writer of great versatility and as a remarkable literary artist: possibly the best Canadian fiction writer before the 1930s. That title has often been given to Frederick Philip Grove, but Duncan showed a mastery of prose style that Grove could not even approach, and her psychological intuitions were far superior to his, even if she did not share his ability to give his visions a Teutonic kind of quasi-mystical portentousness. No novel that Grove wrote was as well constructed or as completely realized as *The Imperialist* or *His Honour, and a Lady*, and Grove's fictional philosophizing seems ponderous and elephantine compared with the sure-handed deftness with which Duncan handled the issues of her day, of which, as a novelist who never ceased to be a journalist, she remained acutely aware and which she approached with a seriousness that was never solemn, so that her occasional didacticism was rarely allowed to destroy the intensity of perception and expression which she treasured.

For Duncan, it must be remembered, started as the contemporary of Oscar Wilde and Walter Pater, even if she survived to meet Forster and to read Aldous Huxley's early novels, and if she never — to my knowledge — quoted Pater's famous dictum, one has the feeling that her intent, even if she did not always sustain it, was to "burn always with the hard, gem-like flame" of discriminating experience. In the process, she contrived to live what was, for a writer, an almost exemplary life: professionally devoted, avid for impressions, and always receptive to the gifts of existence. No Canadian writer before her, and few after her, produced a group of books equivalent to her best: *The Imperialist, The Simple Adventures of a Memsahib, His Honour, and a Lady, The Burnt Offering*, and *Cousin Cinderella*.

The long neglect of Duncan, continued until very recently, was the result of a stifling kind of Canadian parochialism that for many years tended to reject books by Canadians which did not concern Canada. Duncan flouted this attitude, first by frankly declaring her admiration for American novelists and assiduously cultivating the acquaintanceship of writers like Howells and James, and then by departing before she was thirty for her long residence in India. Even before she went, Duncan tended to take as her field of writing the whole world, which she encompassed on long, journalistic voyages, and to project herself into un-Canadian situations and un-Canadian characters, as if she were testing the limits of fictional self-transformation, so that she would write about Americans in England, with more satiric bite than James had used, and about the English in India. Her only book on Canada, *The Imperialist*, appeared in 1904, long after she had left Canada, and her one book about a Canadian abroad, *Cousin Cinderella*, four years later in 1908. Had she stayed at home, and written as well about Canada as she did about India, she would have been as much an accepted figure as Leacock and Gordon became.

The contrast between Duncan's fate and that of Mavis Gallant tells us a great deal about the change in Canadian critical attitudes over recent years, for there is much in common between these two writers, in their perceptions of the visible world as well as in their self-imposed exiles, and yet, though Gallant has mainly published in a single American magazine, *The New Yorker*, as well as living constantly abroad and writing mostly about people dwelling in Europe, she has been generously acclaimed here. In the case of Duncan, the long neglect is only just ending. More than fifty years after her death in 1922, only one of her novels — *The Imperialist* — was available. Recently, however, a number of her books have been reissued, so that now no less than six of her fiction titles are available, though only two of them, *The Imperialist* and the Penguin *The Pool in the Desert*, are in popular and widely distributed editions, while one of her best books, *His Honour, and a Lady*, still remains unavailable. And Thomas E. Tauskey has written his excellent pioneer study *Sara Jeannette Duncan, Novelist of Empire*.

From the beginning, Stephen Leacock never lacked an audience, and even if many of the thirty-five books of humour he published over an obsessively industrious life are no longer available, a surprising number are still in print. Like Gordon's, Leacock's success was a popular one. While he was alive, serious critics hardly noticed him, and although some of his work, like *Literary Lapses*, had a slightly pedantic flavour of donnish jesting, he has been enjoyed much more over the years by the common reader than by the literati, who only comparatively recently have taken him over and used his work to prove theories about irony as "the natural Canadian voice."

Leacock worked hard for his popular success, keeping up a constant flow of jesting sketches to satisfy his readers and placate his own sense of insecurity, but there is the other side of his literary career that is usually neglected even by the critics who have recently taken him up: the popular histories and the expositions of economics for the plain man. Ralph Curry has rightly drawn our attention to this side of Leacock, which meant as much to the writer as his humorous pieces, and, by treating the work as a whole, has shown that there is a real consistency about it.

The clue to that consistency is, I suggest, that like most humorists (though unlike most satirists, who tend to be aristocratically minded), Leacock was a kind of populist, mocking in his comic sketches and essays the establishments that are the common man's enemy, but at the same time making the history of his country and the way its economy works clear to the ordinary reader, who has no taste for footnoted volumes written in the academic jargon which Leacock — like most true scholars — despised.

It was in this common touch, and in the lack of ferocity in his humour, that I think the secret of Leacock's lasting success can be found. Like Charlie Chaplin, he was in his own way the champion of the little man who is without pretensions and who resents the pretensions of others, yet who wishes his presence in the world to be acknowledged. As Curry remarks:

> If one may speak of Leacock's work — in contrast to Leacock's works — his concern and even affection for the common man's desire to be "a name and not a number," to make, and be, a difference, is the single thread on which are strung the separate pieces from his pen. From this, too, we may presently infer the "kindliness" of Leacock's humour.[2]

The difference between Leacock and Gordon, in terms of their popularity, is that Leacock's reputation has survived and even spread to the literati, whereas Gordon, whose works were once on millions of Canadian shelves, is nowadays read neither for entertainment nor for edification, and certainly not for literary mastery, but occasionally by some critic as a historical curiosity. The reasons for this situation lie partly in the differences of literary quality between the two writers, but partly also in shifts in reading patterns, which have made muscular Christianity and Western adventure unfashionable, yet, at the same time, have not diminished the peculiar Canadian taste for what is broadly called humour but should probably be called wit, and which, in our day, can range from the mild and rather Leacockian jesting of an Eric Nicol to the somewhat more savage — but never wholly outrageous — caricatures in words in which Allan Fotheringham embodies his political criticisms. The sun has long set on the great days of American humour from which Leacock derived so much of his inspiration, but in this, as in other matters, Canada tends to be more conservative, and so Leacock is still given his due as a humorist and retains a modest popular esteem even while the serious critics ponder the nature of his talent, and, indeed, the definition of his works.

For it has often been observed that even *Sunshine Sketches of a Little Town*, with its episodic structure and its population of humours rather than characters, is in no true and developed sense a novel. Nor are its episodes short stories that bear any real resemblance to the complex fictional artefacts of Alice Munro or Clark Blaise. They are, as the title frankly tells us, sketches, and the exaggeration, the parody, the incongruity, which become virtually structural principles in their composition, distinguish them from the mainstream of Canadian novel writing, though one can find suggestive resemblances to Leacock in some of the recent meta-fictional novels where the very kind of play with forms one finds in *Literary Lapses* is more complexly carried on.

But combined with the sheer play with literary forms and social situations that constituted the humorous side of Leacock's sketches, there is also the moralistic side, which one can link up with the other — and openly didactic — Leacock of the histories and the books of popular economics. For each of the sketches is constructed to tell us, however obliquely, something about life, about society, about human relations. Some of them are, frankly, essays, bringing Leacock once again, as in the case of his humour, to a characteristic Canadian literary mode, for a surprising number of our writers, even when they succeeded in fiction, remained attracted to the personal essay, and some of these — including Sara Jeannette Duncan, Robertson Davies, Hugh MacLennan, Roderick Haig-Brown, and Hugh Hood — have done surprisingly well in the genre. Thus, because he was a man of letters much concerned with literary artistry as well as a successful popular writer, Leacock shares many of the continuing concerns and inclinations which Canadian writers have displayed down to the present day, and that is one reason why we still read him.

Conversely, it is his lack of overriding concern for the art of writing that really explains why we no longer read Charles Gordon. It is true that, delving through his books, one finds occasional set pieces of scenic description that are lovingly done and have a certain orotund grandeur, but these do not make up for the pretentious and self-righteous prose style, the shallowness of characterization, the plots forced to doctrinally acceptable conclusions, the violence pietistically justified, and the general sense that these are books in which entertainment is used relentlessly for edification and that aesthetic considerations are not merely ignored by the author but are unknown to him.

Even what the *Literary History of Canada* calls Gordon's "fine descriptions of many varied phases of the life of the early settlers"[3] are mainly admirable for their documentary vividness, and they belong properly to social history rather than to literature. The only feasible critical approach to Gordon is a descriptive one, telling us what he sets out to do and how he does it, and this is the approach John Lennox wisely took in his essay on him. Any attempt at evaluative criticism or even at serious textual analysis might have been disastrous, though Freud on Gordon would have been interesting, for there is a great deal of not very deeply repressed homosexuality in Gordon's novels, and the spectre of Oedipus hovers near.

Indeed, best-selling authors like Gordon find their way into literary history less for their actual books, which rapidly fade in significance once the time for which they seemed so appropriate is past, than for what their vogue tells us about what popular audiences needed and got from books in an age before radio and television. As Clara Thomas has remarked:

> It was [Charles Gordon's] fortune that his own imaginings answered perfectly the requirements of a very large number of men and women of his time. Even into the thirties, he had a loyal following that in Canada far outnumbered the potential readership for newer and more seriously artistic novelists. He was, of course, telling the story over and over again, from many angles and in many guises, of the frontier hero and his mate. In each one, readers could see themselves and their choices heightened, glamourized and simplified; they could also live vicariously in worlds of action, danger, hardship, conflict, often cruelty and always adventure — with a comfortable knowledge that in this world the right would, finally, always triumph — and that their author was triumphantly and reassuringly certain, always, of where the "right" lay.[4]

Gordon's novels should be required reading for Canadian social historians, but his place in a serious critical work such as this is at best marginal, and justifiable only because he was present so long and so copiously in Canadian bookstores and on Canadian book-shelves that the phenomenon calls for an explanation.

There was no kind of artistic development in Gordon's novels. Their purposes remained constant: popular success and the trans-mission of an evangelical Christian view of existence. Gordon found a rough-and-ready form that suited his content, and he was satisfied with it. But Robert Stead, who started off as a would-be popular writer, and was reasonably successful in the role, did develop into something more and eventually moved on from a facile romanticism to become one of the leading representatives of what we call Prairie realism.

Gordon had an early influence on Stead, who knew him during his own boyhood, but it was Stead's good fortune that the mission-ary impulse did not seize him, and so his books were not essentially about salvation on the prairie, but about the prairie itself. He accepted the myth of the West as developed by Gordon, but, as Eric Thompson remarks, instead of a religious or moralistic orientation, ". . . he shows a sturdy secularism, and even practicality, of out-look."[5] Thompson sees two stages in Stead's development: when he abandoned his career as a popular Prairie poet to take up fiction, and when he "virtually abandoned the romantic formulas of storytelling, in order to more fully explore a solitary character." This development brought him to a more rigorous examination of the prairie environment as it actually developed over the years since the first waves of settlement and to a more imaginative assessment of human motivations than Gordon had ever attempted.

It is true that not until his third-last novel, *Grain* (1926), did Stead really find himself — and produce a single work that became a Canadian classic — before the atmosphere of Ottawa bureaucracy invaded his mind and effectively destroyed him as a writer, for, after *Grain* appeared, he lived on for thirty-three years and published only one other novel — an undistinguished crime story called *The Copper Disc* (1931). During the mid-1930s, he wrote another Western novel, *Dry Water*, but though he seems to have revised it more than once in the hope of finding a publisher, it did not appear until 1983, twenty-four years after Stead's death, and then added nothing to his reputation. The lapse into uninspired work and, by the 1940s, into silence remains difficult to understand. It may have been nothing more than the change in environment after he moved to Ottawa in 1919 that gradually sapped the immediacy of his memories of the West and left him with nothing else that concerned him strongly enough to write about.

Be that as it may, *Grain* and its central character, Gander Stake, continue to glow with the kind of authentic, unmelodramatic life that Gordon never achieved in his many novels. The romantic touch is not wholly abandoned, for Gander is a creature of obscure, irrational visions, but this modification of strict realism is perhaps to the novel's advantage, combining with an extraordinary authenticity of background to make it one of the best works of fiction to come out of the Prairies before *As for Me and My House* was published in 1941.

Its advocates make bold claims for *Grain*; John Moss calls it "a classic example of prairie realism with more authentic detail of the agrarian life than all the words of Grove put together, with a more coherent social vision of the west than any of [Edward A.] McCourt's novels, and with an even more complete coincidence of land and personality than *Wild Geese*."[6] These are high claims, but they have their own truth, provided one also bears in mind that Stead's prose was rarely better than serviceable, and that no other character he created was as well-rounded and entirely convincing as Gander Stake. But at least, unlike Gordon, Stead realized that good fiction is an art and not entirely a didactic device, and in one novel came near to mastering it completely. A modest achievement, perhaps, compared with the accomplished oeuvres of Duncan and Leacock, but a genuine one.

NOTES

[1] Roy Daniells, "Glengarry Revisited," *Canadian Literature*, No. 31 (Winter 1967), p. 53.

[2] "Stephen Leacock and His Works," in *Canadian Writers and Their Works*, ed. Robert Lecker, Jack David, and Ellen Quigley, Fiction ser., III (Toronto: ECW, 1988), pp. 181–82; hereafter cited as *CWTW*.

[3] Gordon Roper, S. Ross Beharriell, and Rupert Schieder, "Writers of Fiction 1880–1920," in *Literary History of Canada: Canadian Literature in English*, 2nd ed., gen. ed. and introd. Carl F. Klinck (Toronto: Univ. of Toronto Press, 1976), I, 337.

4 Clara Thomas, " 'Ralph Connor' (Charles Gordon)," in *Our Nature — Our Voices: A Guidebook to English-Canadian Literature* (Toronto: new, 1972), pp. 52–53.

5 *CWTW*, Fiction ser., III, p. 222.

6 John Moss, *A Reader's Guide to the Canadian Novel* (Toronto: McClelland and Stewart, 1981), p. 262.

CHAPTER 4

The Rural Realists:
Frederick Philip Grove,
Sinclair Ross, Martha Ostenso,
Raymond Knister, W.O. Mitchell

WITH THE WRITERS discussed in this essay we are probing down to the bedrock of significant Canadian fiction as we have known it for the past generation or so; a tradition founded in realism but ready to learn from modernist and post-modernist innovatory techniques in so far as they sustain that curious combination of goals — verisimilitude tempered by moralism and flavoured at times with Gothic fantasy and talltale exaggeration — that has distinguished the main line of Canadian fiction.

It was long a commonplace of literary history that the Canadian realist tradition emerged in the Prairies, and another commonplace that it represents the principal contribution to Canadian literature of the three provinces that lie between the Shield and the Rockies. And there is enough truth in both views to make them worth examination.

Four out of the five novelists now discussed lived in and wrote of the Prairies, and between them Grove and Ross, Ostenso and Mitchell present in their works a notably large proportion of the interesting Canadian fiction being written between 1925, when Grove published *Settlers of the Marsh*, and 1947, when W.O. Mitchell's *Who Has Seen the Wind* appeared. Any list of Canadian literary classics inevitably includes these two titles as well as Ross's *As for Me and My House*, Ostenso's *Wild Geese*, and certainly at least two of Grove's other titles, *Over Prairie Trails*, his least flawed book, and *The Master of the Mill*. But, as has been pointed out, these four writers represent a much larger range of novelists who wrote out of the Prairie experience during the same period.

Stanley Atherton, writing on Martha Ostenso, reminds us of the popularity of the Prairies in the earlier nineteenth century as a setting for romantic adventure, presented in novels by writers like Gilbert Parker and James Oliver Curwood, Harold Bindloss and Ralph Connor. And he also notes that:

> Another interesting development in the decade preceding the publication of *Wild Geese* was an evolution in the *kind* of fiction produced by a number of Prairie writers. Both Douglas Durkin and Robert Stead began by writing romances, but were later able to make the transition to more serious realistic work.[1]

In fact, the last two writers mentioned by Atherton bear serious comparison with the four Prairie writers included in this chapter; Durkin's *The Magpie* and Stead's *The Smoking Flax* and *Grain* are capable and even powerful works, not inferior to much of Grove or to Sinclair Ross's less successful novels. And Durkin — as Atherton reminds us and as Peter E. Rider originally revealed in introducing a 1974 reprint of *The Magpie* — must take at least part of the credit for *Wild Geese*, which was the result of a collaboration between him and Ostenso and was fraudulently presented as the latter's work to win a literary competition for unpublished writers and for which Durkin, whose major novel had already appeared, was ineligible.

Apart from the writers noted by Atherton, Dick Harrison, discussing W.O. Mitchell[2] also identifies "a more popular if generally less distinguished stream of Prairie fiction in the sentimental comedies of such writers as John Beames, Ross Annett, and Ralph Allen, which have logical antecedents in the sentimental romances of Nellie McClung," and he sees Mitchell's *Who Has Seen the Wind* "as the culmination of that type of fiction, a counterpart in the comic mode to Ross's . . . *As for Me and My House*."[2]

This rich and complex pattern of Prairie fiction has, of course, continued into our own period with the work of writers as important in the general Canadian literary landscape as Margaret Laurence, Rudy Wiebe, and Robert Kroetsch. These younger writers openly acknowledge the importance of their predecessors and the way their own work has been influenced by Grove and Ostenso and Ross, so that there is the sense of a continuing and consciously sustained succession that changes and develops but retains certain basic elements, notably the varying combination of realism and romance that since the 1920s has been characteristic of the fictional genres in a Western setting.

This tradition of Prairie fiction had undoubtedly contributed greatly to Canadian fiction, as a clearly defined regional tradition, and through its more important writers, like Sinclair Ross and Margaret Laurence, its influence has permeated far beyond the Prairies. Academic critics, indeed, tend to become so fascinated by the phenomenon of the least urban area of the country making so impressive a contribution that they tend to exaggerate the importance of the writers who represent it. Perhaps the most striking instance is that of Frederick Philip Grove, about whom there is a curious division of views. Professional writers, being highly craft conscious, are inclined to see Grove's faults very clearly and to regard him at worst as a pretentious bore and at best — to use my own past words which W.J. Keith quotes in his excellent temperate essay — as "a fumbling giant among novelists," who presents us with "the problem of why a writer, so large in texture, so gigantic in his fumblings, never wrote a book that seemed completely to fulfil his possibilities."[3]

Grove has become more interesting to writers since Douglas Spettigue's revelations of his past as Felix Paul Greve, the minor German decadent who faked suicide to escape from a life of crushing indebtedness and from the stigma of imprisonment, but it is as a complex and enigmatic personality that Greve-Grove appeals without the professional view of his quality as a writer having greatly changed.

Academic critics, on the other hand, have made surprising claims. Writing at the time of Grove's death in 1948, Northrop Frye expressed the opinion that "Frederick Philip Grove was certainly the most serious of Canadian prose writers, and may well have been the most important one also."[4] (One wonders in quite what way he was more "serious" as a prose writer than contemporaries like, say, Morley Callaghan or Hugh MacLennan, who were just as much involved in the problems of prose style and in their own ways equally philosophically inclined.) And as late as 1970, at a time when Canadian writing had shown an astonishing degree of vitality and a remarkable qualitative development, Desmond Pacey could still astonishingly remark: "I believe it is true to say that, at home, Grove is regarded as Canada's greatest novelist."[5]

Just as there has been a tendency to inflate Grove's merits largely because of the admirable grandeur of the ambitions he so imperfectly fulfilled in his novels, there is a tendency, I believe, to exaggerate the importance of Prairie fiction in the development of the special kind of realism that is the dominant mode of Canadian fiction. In fact, of course, the growingly recognized presence of Sara Jeannette Duncan, writing through the 1890s and the Edwardian era, undermines the claims that have been made for Grove as the first important Canadian novelist, while her sharp perceptions of Canadian small town life and of turn-of-the-century political prac- tices in *The Imperialist* suggest that there were other sources as well as the Prairie experience for the development of a realist trend in Canada.

There is also, of course, Raymond Knister, whose single success- ful novel, *White Narcissus*, dealt like the Prairie novelists with farming life, and did so, like so many of them, with realism tempered with romantic sentiments. But Knister was writing, not of the homesteads of Prairie pioneers, but of the long-established farms of Ontario. Knister was roughly Grove's contemporary in terms of publication, even if he was twenty years younger in terms of age, and like the older novelist he produced his share of novels too incompletely realized ever to achieve publication. Knister was a young writer of great brilliance and potentiality, and what he might have done if he had not achieved romantic status as Canada's drowned poet, dead at 33, it is hard to prophesy. He might well have started a tradition of Ontario rural writing; he might have developed over a long life into a poet as important as his friend and contemporary, Dorothy Livesay. Apart from his fiction and poetry, he aspired to being the complete man-of-letters, and at times he showed a notable critical acuity.

Among Knister's essays is one on Grove, written in 1928, which is interesting because it gives us a cross reference between contem- poraries and shows a writer who was himself struggling to master the novel as a form recognizing the problems that a fellow novelist encounters. Knister praised *Over Prairie Trails*, which must have appealed to his lyrical sensibility, as "a superb evocation of the prairie winter, sketched in appropriately huge strokes." But he then went on to say, in one of the best comments made by a contemporary:

> It is surprising . . . to find Mr. Grove's novels on the whole so unsatisfactory. "Settler's of the Marsh" is powerfully conceived, the honesty and forthright intentions of the author are apparent, yet the book as a whole misses that finality of effect which it should have. In some instances it is downright awkward and childish, as when every few pages we are shown the depravity of the "fallen woman" the hero has married by the fact that she plasters her face with powder. One cannot help conclude that the novel is a strange harness to Mr. Grove's talent. He has to leave so many things unsaid, and forego the advantage of so many branches of his varied learning, that the finished novel must seem a very fragmentary thing.[6]

That last phrase — "that the finished novel must seem a very fragmentary thing" — is especially acute, for what strikes another writer about Grove is that, just as Lowry would spend years working on novels and yet be quite unable to complete them, so Grove would spend vast amounts of time writing and cutting and shaping, and yet could rarely end up with a book that seemed properly integrated. It was not merely a matter of a rough surface, such as some sculptors deliberately leave, but of structural problems unresolved and which for some deep inner reason Grove seems to have been incapable of resolving. But all this Knister expressed with gentleness and understanding, and in a very different way from the other cross reference between authors that immediately comes to mind in the context of this volume, when Grove, combining the arrogance and the envy that were his two besetting faults, burst out, when *Wild Geese* won its award and Ostenso-Durkin became a best-selling team almost overnight, "only trash wins a prize," which did not prevent him from enjoying his own Governor-General's Award.

Yet the fact that the role of Prairie novelists in Canadian fiction as a whole, and also the importance of some individual Prairie novelists, may have been overstated by academic critics more impressed by a writer's themes than by his way with words, does not lessen the interest of the phenomenon of Prairie fiction. Why did so many good novelists, when one considers the whole succession from Stead to Kroetsch, come out of the Prairies? And why was prose fiction so attractive to Prairie writers, for so many years, to the virtual exclusion of poetry, so that there was no Prairie poet of any consequence between Charles Mair in the 1860s and Eli Mandel in the 1950s?

The two questions are clearly related, and a clue to answering them can perhaps be found in some remarks by Henry Kreisel, centring on Sinclair Ross's *As for Me and My House*, which Morton L. Ross quotes in an essay on his namesake. "All discussion of the literature produced in the Canadian west must of necessity begin with the impact of the landscape on the mind," says Kreisel, and he goes on: "It is because *As for Me and My House* contains the most uncompromising rendering of the puritan state of mind produced on the prairie that the novel has been accorded a central place in prairie literature."[7]

The equation that produces puritan consciousness out of Prairie landscape is one with many and subtle ramifications, for there is no doubt that the best novels of all the four western writers discussed in this volume are haunted by the puritan state of mind, at times to the extent of nightmare. Grove's novels resemble Greek tragedies in the relentlessness of the retribution they offer for human flaws, whether these are mere sensual weaknesses or the lusts for power and wealth. In all Martha Ostenso's Canadian novels the negative and destructive — often ultimately self-destructive — power of the puritan will is evident, and the need to defy it is repeatedly proclaimed. In *As for Me and My House* both of the leading characters are potential artists whose creativity is in every way frustrated by the puritan attitude which affects them in two ways; first, it is part of their own inherited view of life from which they are never able — whatever their doubts and inner rebellions — to escape; beyond that it is the moving spirit of the cruel little town of Horizon in which, for the time of the novel at least, they are obliged to live. Even in the case of W.O. Mitchell, who deliberately turned his talents towards comedy for the greater part of his career, the dread of the natural and instinctual life that is characteristic of the puritan mind was there from the start in the deliberate presentation, even in *Who Has Seen the Wind*, of the passage from innocence to experience as a fall, and the darker implications of this concept of man as a fallen being become much more strongly evident in Mitchell's later novel, *How I Spent My Summer Holidays*, where sexuality becomes an evil, death-ridden force, and the imagery suggests, as I remarked at the time of publication, "a vision that seems to have stepped straight out of the Puritan nightmare."

Perhaps the Prairie novel is the truest manifestation of Northrop Frye's idea of literature in a garrison society. In the vast spaces and the climatic extremes of the great plains, a large number of people, from mainly north European and North American backgrounds, settled in isolated farms or small villages and towns and conquered the land so that its primordial character of a vast open terrain where Indians and bison wandered freely was destroyed, as the survey lines netted it into squared-off farms and the ploughs destroyed the original Prairie vegetation in the same way as the introduction of firearms had destroyed the bison herds and forced the Indians by starvation into accepting a life on reservations.

To conceive such changes required a mentality that could defy nature without and discipline the natural and instinctive elements within men so that work would seem — at least on this earth — their everlasting duty. And the puritan outlook provided that mentality. Whether or not they belonged originally to the traditional puritan sects, those who succeeded on the Prairie were men and women driven by the urge to subdue the land and build a new life there, and in fulfilling that urge the puritan virtues of hard work, self-control, abstemiousness, thrift, were indispensable. It did not make any difference if a man were an Anglican from the English counties, a Scots Presbyterian, a Polish Catholic, or a Ukrainian Orthodox; his share of the puritan virtues was his basic equipment in accepting his tasks as a homesteader, as basic as his plough, and the more stubbornly he continued his struggle with the land, the more the puritan elements were likely to become dominant both in himself and in the society he created. This, I take it, is what Kreisel means by "the puritan state of mind" produced in the Prairie.

But the puritan state of mind in other parts of Canada — in the Maritimes where it flourished greatly and in Upper Canada — was not productive of notable fiction. This is because, I would suggest, nowhere else has it been so strongly involved in its antitheses. Nowhere else in Canada was the struggle with the land so formidable or the land itself, in its sheer open vastness and in the extremity of its natural forces, so antithetical to human desires and intents as in the great plains.

This is why the small towns of Prairie novels, the Manawakas and the Horizons, seem so much like precariously held outposts isolated in the vastness of the land, and why they are such ingrown settlements and so cruel to those who do not abide by the puritan virtues and in this way break the solidarity of the embattled human community. This is why the wind, so relentless in its blowing yet so filled with the scented intimations of another kind of living, plays such an important role in Prairie fiction and in Mitchell's and Ross's novels especially, and why the wild geese that open and close Ostenso's novel, as their haunting cries across the sky intimate the possibility of a free and proud life untrammelled by the puritan urges and inhibitions, stay so firmly in the mind as the guiding symbol as well as the title of the book. That is why the Prairie itself, and especially its untamed recesses, is at once a threat and a temptation.

Perhaps one can regard the realism that is the dominant mode of the Prairie novel as itself a manifestation of the puritan state of mind; it parallels the other kind of "realism" that sets a man solving the practical problems of life with sense, diligence, and not too much sentiment. But there is something hubristic about this puritan "realism." It succeeds only by setting aside as irrelevant both the untamed processes of nature and the instinctual urges within man, and so it serves God by defying the gods. The consequence is that the very forces it had ignored in the end rise up against it. It was the recognition of this conflict, continuing even after the land had been tamed, between "realism" and reality, that set Prairie people writing novels rather than poems and gave those books the agony and intensity that, in the works of writers like Sinclair Ross and Margaret Laurence, have carried them to the forefront of Canadian fiction.

In the process, just as practical "realism" has been attacked, so literary realism has been modified. For the struggle between the instinctual and the dutiful, with all its perversions of tyranny and greed, inevitably tinges realism with romance, even if only in the Lawrencian sense, while the revenges of circumstance, the punishments for hubris, often make inevitable the intrusion of Gothic fantasy.

So we see the Prairie novel, at its best, as one of those mongrel breeds that often show so much more vitality then the purebred strains. It is realist in the sense that it consciously and conscientiously gives us the Godwinian picture of "things as they are," of the struggle to subdue the land and to survive in the process that is man's life on the Prairie, and the way that life shapes and often misshapes both communities and individuals. But it takes its own vitality from the tension between this "reality" and the emotions and aspirations and longings that rebel against it, whether they flourish in the loves frustrated by parental tyranny in Ostenso-Durkin's *Wild Geese* and *The Young May Moon*, or emerge in the frustrated desire to live a creative life that, despite their differences, unites the Bentleys in *As for Me and My House*. And in this sense we can certainly call the Prairie novel romantic.

But there are also elements in Prairie fiction that bring it very close to Gothic fantasy. Margot Northey in *The Haunted Wilderness: The Gothic and Grotesque in Canadian Fiction* has noted "the heightened depiction of life found in some of Frederick Philip Grove's fiction, such as *The Yoke of Life*,"[8] and has enlarged on "the sense of impending catastrophe"[9] that permeates *Wild Geese* and "the mood of menace and terror" induced in that novel by the combination of such factors as "the mysterious and destructive role of nature, and the wilful evil of Caleb Gare."[10] Nothing could be more Gothic in its combination of horror, elemental justice, and underlying absurdity (requiring a hearty "suspension of disbelief") than Caleb's death, swallowed into the liquid mud of a muskeg he should have known well as he hurried to save his blue-flowered field of flax from the onrush of a Prairie fire. There is a touch of lurking menace even in a novel of the Prairies so apparently comic in intent as *Who Has Seen the Wind*, and this certainly descends into "a mood of menace and terror" in Mitchell's later novel, *How I Spent My Summer Holidays*, while the kind of politically oriented Gothicism that flourished in Zamiatin's *We* and George Orwell's *Nineteen Eighty-Four* found a not unworthy congener on Grove's *The Master of the Mill*, where the mill becomes a sinister symbol of man's subordination to his own industrial and political systems.

There is a special kind of seriousness, a moral earnestness, in the more important Prairie novels, that tends to make critics treat them with a respect that demands more than mere formal analysis or aesthetic appreciation. These are writers out to tell us something about life and the way it should and/or should not be lived; their content emphatically demands our attention, even when they are not being tediously didactic, as they sometimes are. We read them with the sense that we are going to learn something as well as gaining imaginative satisfaction, and we are rarely disappointed. Grove was in a way the exception among them in starting off as the aesthete Greve, a devotee of Wilde and the other Decadents, but it would have surprised his early and rather dismissive acquaintance, André Gide, to see him turning into perhaps the most determined moralist, posing earnest questions about existence, of all the Prairie writers. The problem of freedom and determination lies at the heart of Grove's work, endlessly developed in changing permutations. In the first of his novels to be published, *Settlers of the Marsh*, he poses the question:

> Are there in us unsounded depths of which we do not know ourselves? Can things outside of us sway us in such a way as to change our very nature? Are we we? Or are we mere products of circumstance?[11]

It is a question that seems to have lurked in the minds of many of the Prairie novelists, deriving naturally from that "impact of the landscape on the mind" to which Kreisel also attributes the prevalence of the puritan mentality in the Prairies. To this extent the vestiges of the naturalist heritage are evident not only in Grove. But they are balanced by the defiant sense that liberty is possible and that, if it is not, the injustice is monstrous, so that whatever quasi-naturalist presentation of existence-as-it-is we find among these writers is balanced by the sense that even in the flat monotonies of the Prairie, man can stand upright and free in the challenging wind.

It is, I believe, the recognition of this uncompromising seriousness — which made even W.O. Mitchell seem in the end a tragic rather than a comic novelist — that explains the careful and sensible quality of the essays included in this chapter. They all add notably to the discussions carried on up to now in relation to the novelists they concern.

W.J. Keith's sympathies for Grove are obvious and multiple in their origins. Like Grove and Wyndham Lewis and me, he came out of a European background into a Canadian literary world whose denizens were not always welcoming. I remember the bitter attack made on his excellent study of Charles G.D. Roberts by a nationalist poetaster too paltry to name, merely because Keith was British by origin. And so I see in context his excellent statement why we should consider Grove seriously as introducing a new element into the Canadian literary landscape.

> Instead of the standard classical education of, say, the "Confederation Poets," Grove enjoyed a deeper understanding of the whole European tradition; instead of an American-based, contemporary-oriented narrowness of attitude, he brought a consciousness personally aware of the artistic achievements and experiments of continental Europe, a familiarity with other literary movements, an openness to new creative possibilities.[12]

Keith's interest in rural literature, which had led to some excellent studies in the English country-writing tradition, has given him a good deal of insight into Grove as a kind of agrarian novelist, and the admiration for Wordsworth he has often expressed also fits into context, for Wordsworth too was one of those ponderous and loquacious writers with broad philosophic content who form a large image in the mind but whose air of the majestic is never completely convincing because their way with words is never sharp or deft enough. Both need the distillation neither was able to perform of his own works.

Perhaps it is the multiplicity of these sympathies that explains why Keith has been able to express his admiration for Grove, which is clearly considerable, in a temperate yet sympathetic way that consistently engages one's interest. Certainly he hits upon an important insight into the achievement of that notable liar paradoxically dedicated to the pursuit of artistic truth when at the end of his essay he talks of Desmond Pacey's use of the word "Integrity," at first sight rather surprisingly, in describing Grove.

Integrity! The word seems strange after the revelations of the "sullied" European years. Yet it is a word that commentators on Grove constantly find themselves needing to use (similarly, I wrote of his "sincerity of purpose" three paragraphs back). Here, perhaps, a gleam of light is shed upon the artistic implications of the so-called Grove mystery. The firm literary integrity pervading the work of Frederick Philip Grove, though ironically including a deceiving account of his own development, seems to have been a massive act of redemption offered as personal penance for the moral shortcomings in the life of Felix Paul Greve. And Canadian fiction is richer as a consequence.[13]

Perhaps, indeed, the process of redemption had already begun in Germany after the prison interlude, when Felix Paul Greve in fact initiated the career of Frederick Philip Grove by writing those early novels, *The Master Mason's House* and *Fanny Essler*, which in a number of important ways anticipated the fiction of the Canadian years.

Recent research has revealed unfamiliar aspects of Martha Ostenso's past as well as Frederick Philip Grove's, though the revelations in her case have not been so bizarre as in Greve-Grove's. Not long ago it was generally assumed that her novels were her own unaided work; the general ignorance about her was linked to an inclination to regard her as a novelist who wrote only one really successful work and at the same time only one novel of interest to Canadians. Even the entry on Ostenso in the 1983 *Oxford Companion to Canadian Literature* mentions only *Wild Geese*, though the author, Joy Kuropatwa, is aware of Ostenso's collaboration with Durkin and remarks that she published "over a dozen volumes of fiction."[14] In fact Ostenso and Durkin wrote sixteen novels, and three of them, beside *Wild Geese*, have Canadian settings, including what is probably the best of her later novels, *The Young May Moon*, also set in Manitoba, as well as *Prologue to Love* and *The White Reef*, both of which have British Columbian backgrounds. It is also clear that her Canadian experience and that of Durkin influenced notably the later novels published under Ostenso's name, even when their settings were American, and that Canada continued to attract her, so that there has been a certain injustice in her having been seen for so long by Canadians as if she were important merely for a single book. By examining her career as a whole, Stanley Atherton has not merely shown that some of her later works were a good deal more than pot-boilers; he has also restored to our attention one excellent novel about Canadian Prairie life, *The Young May Moon*, and one hopes his essay will be the beginning of a broader appreciation of the results of the Ostenso-Durkin joint work and perhaps a closer study of the real nature of the collaboration.

As Atherton convincingly argues, Ostenso-Durkin wrote at least two other books that can stand beside the better-known *Wild Geese*. In the case of Sinclair Ross, it is harder to break the image of an essentially one-novel writer, for though Morton L. Ross has given fair treatment to all of Sinclair Ross's books, one is still left after reading his essay, as one is after repeatedly reading the Sinclair Ross *oeuvre*, with the knowledge that, apart from a few of his early short stories, Ross wrote nothing afterwards even nearly equal to *As for Me and My House*. Perhaps one can find the reason for this inability to repeat an early triumph in Ross's removal from his Prairie background almost from the time his first novel was published. But such creative intermittencies are as mysterious as the creative process itself, of which Sinclair Ross himself wrote cagily and sensibly in the 1970 essay quoted by Morton Ross and entitled "On Looking Back," in which he refused to talk about his "sensibility and creative processes," arguing that:

> . . . artists themselves as well as psychologists seem pretty well agreed that the "creative sources" are in the subconscious, and the psychologists are also agreed that self-analysis can seldom do more than scrape the surface. . . . So if I don't understand myself — my "creative processes" if you like, why I did this and that — how could I possibly write about them?[15]

From personal experience and from observing many writers who are my friends, I can only agree with Ross. The so-called artists who can explain their creative impulses are usually at best artificers. And this is why I welcome Morton Ross's attempt to restore a measure of respect for the artists' lack of deliberation in his discussion of the aspect of *As for Me and My House* that the academic critics have worn threadbare — the reliability and, indeed, the integrity of the narrator of the novel, Mrs. Bentley.

I enter on this subject with some caution, since the matter was brought into the open by two critics who are my friends and were indeed my associates in editing *Canadian Literature*, Donald Stephens and W.H. New. Donald Stephens rightly warned us against accepting Mrs. Bentley's narrative at face value; in doing so he was laying emphasis on the subjectivity of point of view with which one cannot disagree. W.H. New entered a more perilous area by arguing, in Morton Ross's words, "that the deliberate aim of the novel is ambivalence" emerging (and here we use New's own words) "out of a carefully constructed web of viewpoints, Mrs. Bentley's and ours, pitted ironically against each other so that we come to appreciate not only the depth and complexity of the narrator and her situation, but also the control in which Ross artistically holds his words." To that I must answer, with the suspicion that I would have Sinclair Ross's support, that the "deliberation" which critics often attribute to writers exists usually only in the critic's mind, and that the "carefully constructed web of viewpoints" is more likely to be a clustering of intuitive insights that comes together in the writer's mind as he is actually working, often fully formed, and is probably only in a slight degree a product of the deliberating intelligence. Novels are not mathematical propositions. Rather than seeking the origins of Mrs. Bentley's ambivalences in artifice, I would suggest they are the products of a writer's naturally ironic sensibility operating in a situation given by the imagination. Those who see Ross as exposing Mrs. Bentley to our contempt are mistaken; he is rather developing out of his natural awareness of human psychology the ways in which the mind can combine clear perception with self-deception without being entirely aware of the distinction. In Mrs. Bentley as in all of us weaknesses and virtues are combined, and in the confusion of them — and the occasional perception of that confusion — lies the ironic structure of the novel — of which, despite her preoccupations with her husband Philip, she remains the centre. Morton Ross's debate with Mrs. Bentley's denigrators helps us understand this.

In more than one way, Mitchell is the most divided if not exactly the most complex of the novelists studied here. He belongs in appearance to the "popular" comic tradition of Prairie writing as distinct from the "serious" tragic one, and the corpus of his writing shows that curious combination of the passing and the permanent that develops with any writer who has committed himself over a long period to turning out radio and television scripts which, because of their very form, are unpublishable and — except in an archival sense — perishable.

What is perhaps most impressive about Mitchell, and what Harrison admirably traces, is the way in which, despite his comic beginnings, despite his popularity as a radio and television writer, despite his folksy public personality, Mitchell found himself drawn into the mainstream of Prairie writing, and in doing so allowed the tragic intimations that were always present in his work to surface and become dominant. Perhaps more strikingly than any other example, the transformation of W.O. Mitchell shows the unity of Prairie fiction as a tradition of its own within Canadian literature.

NOTES

1 "Martha Ostenso and Her Works," in *Canadian Writers and Their Works*, ed. Robert Lecker, Jack David, and Ellen Quigley, Fiction ser., IV (Toronto: ECW, 1991), p. 216; hereafter cited as *CWTW*.

2 *CWTW*, Fiction ser., IV, p. 145.

3 George Woodcock, "Editorial," *Canadian Literature*, No. 29 (Spring 1966), p. 4; *Odysseus Ever Returning: Essays on Canadian Writers and Writing* (Toronto: McClelland and Stewart, 1970), pp. 3–4, 149.

4 Northrop Frye, "Canadian Dreiser," *The Canadian Forum*, Sept. 1948, p. 121.

5 Desmond Pacey, Introd., *Frederick Philip Grove*, ed. Desmond Pacey (Toronto: Ryerson, 1970), p. 1.

6 Raymond Knister, "Frederick Philip Grove," *Ontario Library Review*, 13 (1928), 62.

7 Henry Kreisel, "The Prairie: A State of Mind," *Transactions of the Royal Society of Canada*, 4th ser., 6 (June 1968), 173.

8 Margot Northey, *The Haunted Wilderness: The Gothic and Grotesque in Canadian Fiction* (Toronto: Univ. of Toronto Press, 1976), p. 62.

9 Northey, p. 63.

10 Northey, p. 65.

11 Frederick Philip Grove, *Settlers of the Marsh*, New Canadian Library, No. 50 (Toronto: McClelland and Stewart, 1966), p. 166.

[12] *CWTW*, Fiction ser., IV, p. 25.

[13] *CWTW*, Fiction ser., IV, pp. 57–58.

[14] Joy Kuropatwa, "Ostenso, Martha," in *The Oxford Companion to Canadian Literature*, ed. William Toye (Toronto: Oxford Univ. Press, 1983), p. 626.

[15] Sinclair Ross, "On Looking Back," *Mosaic*, 3, No. 3 (Spring 1970), 94.

CHAPTER 5

A Transitional Generation:
Hugh MacLennan, Morley Callaghan,
Thomas Raddall, Ernest Buckler,
Howard O'Hagan

POETRY is on the whole more quickly responsive to the shifts in general consciousness than fiction, perhaps because the lyric and the elegiac modes are largely dependent on the crystallization of the immediate impression, whether it is an emotion or an image. Fiction, from the mere fact that it takes longer to gestate, tends to relate itself to deeper and slower changes in collective sensibilities and attitudes. It is rather like the relation between the *plein air* sketch and the studio painting, or the snapshot and the daguerro-type. And so it is not surprising that the development in Canadian fiction did not really begin much before the 1930s. In a similar way, genuinely experimental poetry was being written in the late 1920s by poets like W.W.E. Ross and Dorothy Livesay and A.J.M. Smith, while — with the exception of Howard O'Hagan's disregarded *Tay John* in 1939 — it is hard to think of a genuinely experimental Canadian novel before Sheila Watson's *The Double Hook* in 1959.

However, the cases of poetry and fiction are parallel in the sense that, for both, there was a transition between the recognition of the need for a literature that springs from local or national experience and which is new in the sense of its changed objectives and material, and the development of the experimental forms that bespeak a new voice as well as a new perception. In this sense the writers which this volume includes — Hugh MacLennan, Morley Callaghan, Thomas Raddall, Howard O'Hagan, and Ernest Buckler — resemble the so-called Confederation Poets who started to work roughly half a century before. With their Western contemporaries like F.P.

Grove, Martha Ostenso, and the slightly earlier Robert J.C. Stead, they represent a transitional generation that is important at least as much for its intent as for its achievement. It is arguable that there are earlier Canadian novelists as capable as any of those discussed here, such as James De Mille and Sara Jeannette Duncan, but those writers, lacking an adequate local readership and the kind of literary world that might support them, looked outward for publishers and readers and even, like Duncan, sought most of their material in what in those days seemed more interesting settings than the Canadian homeland.

The generation represented here was the first among novelists that turned deliberately to Canada for its material, that found a responsive readership at home and at least the beginnings of an adequate literary infrastructure, and in the process, with varying degrees of deliberation, added a cultural dimension to the transition from a colonial to a national outlook that developed so strongly among Canadians during and between the two world wars.

The five writers are close contemporaries, born within six years of each other: O'Hagan in 1902, Callaghan and Raddall in 1903, MacLennan in 1907, and Buckler in 1908. They were all boys during the Great War; they grew into manhood in the roller coaster interbellum years when the false boom of the 1920s gave way to the Depression and World War II, a time of rapidly changing social mores and of political radicalization. Three out of the five are Maritimers, with Torontonian Morley Callaghan and Albertan O'Hagan the exceptions; MacLennan and Raddall shared the Halifax explosion of 1917 as a cataclysmic event of childhood, while MacLennan and Buckler were studying during the same years at Dalhousie University. Finally, all five have adapted to current uses the traditions of romance and realism that had developed by the time they began writing. Formally, in fact, they have been adapters more than they have been imitators.

In the past, I have written extensively on Hugh MacLennan and fairly extensively on Morley Callaghan and I should say at the outset that I appreciate the fairness with which Helen Hoy and Gary Boire respectively have treated my views in their essays[1] on the two novelists, even when they partially or wholly disagreed with them. On Raddall and O'Hagan I have written comparatively little and on Buckler almost nothing, and perhaps for this reason alone it may be appropriate to address my specific remarks first to these writers.

It has been Raddall's fortune and misfortune to succeed as a popular writer. He himself has claimed, as Alan R. Young notes, that "My deep preference . . . would be the writing of history," and there is no doubt that he has been a fine regional historian, presenting well-researched material more vividly and readably than most of his academic rivals. This consideration is not really peripheral to our view of him as a novelist, for his books have been best when he has been guided by his concern for the exactitude of historical background and the plausibility of action, and least good when he departs, as Young rightly notes he does in *The Governor's Lady*, in the direction of "costume romance."[2]

Many critics in the past have treated Raddall as a writer marginal to the mainstream of Canadian literature. Desmond Pacey talks disparagingly of his novels about "fancy-dress personages,"[3] and I myself, as Young recalls, have written negatively about his short stories. If I granted the excellence of the story-telling in his novels about the Nova Scotian past, I also claimed that this kind of excellence in fact placed him "far nearer to writers like Conrad and Robert Louis Stevenson than to Canadian writers of the present generation."[4]

Essentially, the disagreements between the apologists for Raddall and those who consider him a minor writer in terms of the Canadian novelistic tradition rest on the question of the contemporary relevance of well-crafted writing in an obsolete genre, and while Young grants that his "critical assessment . . . largely sides" with the apologists, I find myself among those who are less than convinced about Raddall's lasting importance, at least as a historical novelist.

Young himself brings forward the evidence that establishes Raddall's formal conservatism. The list of fiction writers for whom the novelist expressed admiration and who seem to have influenced him notably — Cooper, Kipling, Stevenson, Conan Doyle, and Conrad — includes, except for Conrad, none of the real writing masters of the age, and modernism of any kind appears to have left him untouched. Young himself also remarks that "frequently Raddall's fiction follows the classic model first established by Scott," and he notes the essential conservatism of the social and political values that the historical novels project.

Young lays the claim that Raddall has been "the most distinguished present-day exponent of the historical romance in Canada," and this may indeed be true. One might even go farther and grant that Raddall, because of his documentary accuracy and his fine story-telling, is in fact among the best of all Canadian historical romancers, certainly far better than Sir Gilbert Parker and his ilk. But the fact seems to remain that, except in popular fiction where it survives in a degenerated form, the historical novel of the kind Raddall has done so well belongs, like its subject matter, to the past, and that, while there has indeed been a revival of historical fiction as a serious genre in the hands of writers like Anthony Burgess and — in Canada — Timothy Findley, it has taken ironical and metafictional directions far removed from Raddall's practice or intent.

But Raddall has not been merely concerned with history in its factual and fictional forms. He has also written three novels of contemporary life, and one of these, *The Nymph and the Lamp*, will probably outlast in interest even the best of his historical novels. Here Raddall calls on experience rather than on research as he creates a memorable image of a Nova Scotian offshore island as a setting for his love triangle, an image so memorable that the island as much as Isabel Jardine, the "nymph," stays intensely in one's memory. As John Moss put it, "Image and symbol merge in this novel quite brilliantly, as do characters and place. The effect is romance, realistically conveyed."[5]

This is hardly the place to go at length into regional differences between fictional approaches, but one cannot help noting that the Nova Scotian novelists tended to be influenced by the traditions of romance while their Prairie contemporaries were more closely dominated by realistic and even — in the case of Grove — by naturalistic inclinations. Both Ernest Buckler and Hugh MacLennan show this romantic tendency, and the difference between them and their Western counterparts may well be due to the fact that in the Prairies during the interbellum, white society was still at the pioneer stage, with not much in the way of a past, whereas Nova Scotians lived with a long history that has played an important role in their literature, for Raddall has been only one among a number of local historical novelists.

Ernest Buckler is not a historical novelist, but a strong sense of the past, and of a settled rural society with its special ways of living and its oral traditions, is never absent from his writings. Douglas Spettigue, in an essay first published in *Canadian Literature* entitled "The Way It Was: Ernest Buckler," points out how recurrent this phrase is in Buckler's writings, how powerful a role reminiscence plays in all his fiction, and how this links his work with one of the constant strains in Canadian writing — that which unites the popular and sentimental rural idyll of the turn of the century with more clearly novelistic forms and often takes the shape of recollections of "childhood scenes set on the farm or in the village and attempting to capture the flavour of a way of life that can no longer be the way it was."[6]

In Buckler's case the simple nostalgia that characterizes many idylls of this kind is complicated by the pull of urban civilization, of the sophisticated culture that has its setting outside the rural community. His own life was largely controlled by this polarity, for, like Paul Creed, the Prospero in his second novel, *The Cruelest Month*, he went away from his rural Nova Scotia to study and to work in Toronto, found that he did not like the life of the city though he was attracted to its culture, and in 1936 returned to the family farm in the Annapolis Valley, where he remained until his death in 1984, living a life of semi-reclusion and devoting himself painstakingly to his writing.

Perhaps it was the reclusion, or perhaps it was the slow elaboration of his books, that served to mark off Buckler's writing so clearly from that of his contemporaries. He was not really interested, though he excelled in evocative description, in the realism to which both MacLennan and Callaghan veered, and he was in no sense a social novelist. Though the actual verses he wrote can only be classed as bad, his stress on symbolism and multiple imagery gave his writing a kind of elegiac poeticism, so that something near to the atmosphere of an idyll was created in which the action tended to be parabolic rather than plausible. A distinct cleavage of approach as a writer mirrored the division in his own mind between the countryman and the sophisticate. He was a regional novelist in the sense of calling up nostalgically a dead or dying rural way of life in a particular locality, yet at the same time he aspired to an early twentieth-century cosmopolitan tradition by making his two novels very near to *Künstlerroman*, books concerned with the emotional wounds that create the artist's peculiar sensibility and in the process detach him from the currents of a "real" life. Thus, the artist manqué, David Canaan, must incur death to obtain his mountaintop moment of transcendental enlightenment, while his grandmother Ellen, secure in the inarticulate traditions of the land, completes her own creation, the many coloured rug made out of the garments of the dead and the living and symbolizing the continuities in human life that proceed outside the artist's vision.

Self-consciousness and its inadequacies are perhaps the main themes of Buckler's second novel, *The Cruelest Month*, whose resemblance to Thomas Love Peacock's conversational novels of manners critics have been slow to observe. In this novel, as Douglas Spettigue remarks, Buckler "examines city people whose complexities are word-shaped, whose pastime is finding the words for their own emotions."[7] In the end, emotions and external events — notably a forest fire started inadvertently by one of the city guests — take precedence over the play of words and ideas, and the guests depart, sadder if not wiser, while Paul Creed, the intellectual whose retreat to the country parallels Buckler's own, finds fulfilment with his illiterate housekeeper, Letty, a simple, shrewd, untalkative countrywoman who resembles the archetypal earth mother.

The taking of pains is evident both in the slow construction of Buckler's novels and in the unusual elaboration of the prose. In a very interesting essay, "The Genesis of Ernest Buckler's *The Mountain and the Valley*,"[8] Alan R. Young demonstrates how Buckler worked over the same material in various ways, eventually constructing *The Mountain and the Valley* largely by adapting previously written stories and fitting them into the larger framework of a novel. Reading this article, one is impressed by the relative narrowness of Buckler's inventiveness in plotting, the comparatively few basic situations that he developed, writing and rewriting and changing from one form to another, over what was after all a long literary career of forty years since his first stories began to appear in the 1940s.

To some Buckler's prose is satisfying because of its richness; to others, as W.J. Keith has remarked, "this way of writing is too cloying."[9] In his essay on Buckler in *Canadian Writers and Their Works*, John Orange defines and defends the novelist's prose:

In his short stories, then, Buckler perceptibly struggles for the exact symbol, word, or figure of speech that will contain both intensity and accuracy of emotion and at the same time focus the story's theme. His prose is influenced by poetry, and like poetry it depends on rhythm, association, and ornamentation of language in order to be both concrete and connotative. Hence we find a proliferation of metaphors, similes, images, conceits, and sound effects (alliteration and assonance) in the prose sentences. The effect of poetic devices inserted into prose is that they slow down the speed of writing and give it a meditative quality. Its primary appeal is to the emotions and to the synthesizing function of the imagination, but it encourages a secondary effect of contemplation, so that it has a metaphysical thrust like that of imagist poetry. Taken too far it becomes euphuism — which is often sentimental, discontinuous, a parody of itself. However, Buckler learned to control his prose by experimenting in his short stories. In his first novel, he brought it to maturity.[10]

I agree with this description of Buckler's early prose in the short stories. But, except for a little tightening and tidying, I see no great difference in *The Mountain and the Valley*. It is written in an over-decorated and over-elaborate manner, lush rather than mature, and Buckler still follows that *ignis fatuus*, a poetic prose, declining to recognize that prose has its values and virtues and does not need to borrow others. As Keith remarks, "the style sets the book apart in a somewhat ambiguous way, rather like David's scar within the narrative itself."[11] Some readers, at least, prefer *The Cruelest Month*, where the very Peacockian structure of conversation and argument assures that here at least we have prose that aspires to be nothing more.

Between the two of them, Hugh MacLennan and a Morley Callaghan emerging from more than a decade of virtual silence tended to dominate the 1950s in Canadian fiction, and of the two, MacLennan, with his clear extra-literary message of Canadian self-realization, was undoubtedly the more widely read and the more influential, so that literary historians have been inclined to refer to the period as the MacLennan decade.

In many ways MacLennan and Callaghan are greatly dissimilar

writers. Their conceptions of the writer's role have differed widely, and so have their styles, both personal and literary. But they have shared throughout their careers a desire to shake free of the domination of the Old World, and this in spite of the fact that MacLennan spent several of his formative years in Oxford and Callaghan did the same in Paris, and also in spite of the profound influence of classical Greek epic and drama on the archetypal structures of MacLennan's fiction.

Callaghan went to the extent of declaring himself in his one autobiographical work, *That Summer in Paris*, to be "intensely North American," and "intellectually, spiritually, . . . but splendidly and happily, alien" to the "very British city" of Toronto.[12] Though he has not been so explicit, MacLennan's constant preoccupation with the development of a Canadian consciousness and with Canada's relationship to the elephantine power that shares a subcontinent with it, implies that he also developed early a North American, as distinct from a narrowly American, consciousness. It would be hard, though the effort has sometimes been made in the case of Callaghan, to slot either of them into a history of American literature, so locally Canadian have been the social and topographical landscapes within which they have mostly developed their fictional visions, while the moral preoccupation of their books carry them beyond the narrow bounds of a continental setting. Both could, I think, be regarded as mental citizens of Canada, which is North American, and of the world, but with no imperial loyalties — to either London or New York — between the local and the global.

Yet both were affected by the literary movements that took place after the Great War in the United States. Like many earlier Canadian writers — James De Mille, John Richardson, etc. — they had found New York a nearer and more receptive market for their books than London, and this was the kind of accident that helped to turn their attention towards the young American writers who seemed to be developing a new literary language that was appropriate to their time and place. And it was perhaps more than coincidence that attracted both of them in their early writing years towards Ernest Hemingway, with his radical stylistic simplification, his power of rendering action in telling prose, and his willingness to face up, without Jamesian circumlocution, to the hard choices of life and death.

Callaghan's involvement with Hemingway was close and personal; he knew him at the *Toronto Star* and later in Paris, and Hemingway not only gave him direct literary advice but also arranged for the first publication of his writings in expatriate periodicals run by American editors. Advice and assistance were accompanied by influence; both the style and the characterization in some of Callaghan's early stories and in an apprentice novel like *Strange Fugitive* are largely derivative from Hemingway, though by the early 1930s Callaghan had shaken off his dependence and was writing his own kind of prose in his own kind of moralist récits.

With MacLennan the influence was much less direct; there are no early passages that can be easily matched with similar passages in Hemingway, as is the case with Callaghan. But he went through an early phase of admiration for Hemingway which was followed during the 1950s by a sharp reaction against the nihilism into which by this time the American writer seemed to him to have descended. Elspeth Cameron, in an essay "Of Cabbages and Kings: The Concept of Hero in *The Watch That Ends the Night*," has very convincingly traced the kind of dialectic by which MacLennan resolved in his largest novel the tension between his admiration and his revulsion for Hemingway, and how he used that resolution "as a springboard to launch a hero he thought reflected the new age"; the hero was not, as might be expected, the obviously Hemingway-esque Jerome Martell, but the almost banal narrator, George Stewart:

> Although the splendid Jerome might seem remote from the lives of average readers because his particular "human condition" was unusually dramatic and his "human spirit" remarkably strong, George Stewart was a man with whom any reader could imaginatively trade places in order to see the importance, the depth and even the beauty of the age-old pattern.[13]

But while it is true that the universality of the age-old pattern is a theme of MacLennan's writings, and that he is constantly warning us about the worldwide collapse of a stable order ("patristic," in his phraseology, as compared with the "matristic" permissiveness he fears and condemns), we still see MacLennan, both in his works themselves and in the remarkably thorough analysis of them Helen

Hoy has given us in her essay, as primarily a social novelist. I have remarked elsewhere that if there is any writer in whose works we can find a Canadian equivalent of Balzac's *La Comédie Humaine*, it is Hugh MacLennan.

Indeed, a cultural historian of Canada dealing with the fifty-odd years between, say 1910 and 1965, could do no better than start with the corpus of MacLennan's works — the seven novels, supplemented by the four hundred essays, slight and serious, dealing with a vast range of the aspects of life and letters in our age. The major areas of Canadian preoccupation over that period are all there: the emergence of a sense of nationhood in *Barometer Rising*; the tension between two cultures in a single land in *Two Solitudes*; the uneasy relationship between Canada and the United States in *The Precipice*; the destructive heritage of ancient religious prejudices in *Each Man's Son*; the bitter awakening from the idealistic dreams of the 1930s in *The Watch That Ends the Night*; the generational conflicts that during the 1960s took negative political forms in Canada as much as any other western country in *The Return of the Sphinx*; the dismal record of political dishonesty and blindness that may doom our civilization in *Voices in Time*; and all supplemented by the multitude of notations on morals and manners and tastes and fashions in the essays.

MacLennan has always been unashamedly didactic; he has always believed that the writer must teach the lessons that are appropriate to his time, and he has always considered the artifice of his novels secondary to the themes. But in the process, rather like his historian counterpart, Donald Creighton, who was also determined to teach lessons about Canadian nationality, he has managed to give a powerful mythical quality to much that he creates. As I and other critics have shown, he has always been ready to appropriate and adapt for his own uses the classical myths he learnt in his youth, of wandering Odysseus and doomed Oedipus, but he can also create his own myths out of contemporary events. His recreation of the Halifax explosion in *Barometer Rising* and his thrilling account of Jerome's flight from his mother's murderer in *The Watch That Ends the Night*, loom over the early decades of the Canadian novel as great examples of powerful writing and high imaginative intensity, and at the same time, as striking symbolic statements.

In a very felicitous comparison, Helen Hoy remarks:

... he is the E.J. Pratt of Canadian fiction, a lone Canadian mythmaker, innovative in his choice of national and "non-literary" subject matter, distinctive in his documentary and social focus, conventional, even old-fashioned, in his choice of form. Too individual to be a model for subsequent writers, MacLennan's work is a turning point in the development of a distinctly national literature.[14]

MacLennan always laid the claim to be mentally slow on the uptake, to be intuitive rather than intellectual, to take a long time to realize the implications of what he was writing, but readers who admire the elaborate didactic structure of his books and the sharp brightness of many of his essays are inclined to be sceptical. On the other hand, it is clear that fictional creation does not come readily to MacLennan. His books take him a long time to produce, since he writes and rewrites, relegating hundreds of thousands of words to the waste-basket or the archives, and reaches the final form only with great effort. He is one of those writers who are made — even self-made — rather than born, and this may perhaps explain the lack of formal originality in his writings. As Hoy points out, his plots tend to be formulaic and melodramatic; he regularly uses the devices of popular romances; his style — particularly when he is dealing with male-female encounters — is, as Hoy remarks, "frequently mawkish and evasive." Younger writers have been inspired by his devotion to solving the problems of Canadian nationality, but nobody has really learnt much from him about the arts of writing and he has had virtually no imitators, even though his novels were sufficiently powerful in their own way to dominate a generation in Canadian fiction, as Pratt's conservative epics did in Canadian poetry.

Morley Callaghan has never figured as a Canadian nationalist, even a literary one, yet, at the time when the temptation to follow a career in the United States must have been great, he elected for Toronto, despite all the features of its life that he disliked. It was a natural instinct that led him, of the same kind that eventually led Mordecai Richler back to Montreal; Toronto was the place where he had grown up and which provided that bank of images a writer accumulates in the first twenty years of his life and afterwards expands only slowly, if at all. The life of the twin cities of central

Canada, Toronto and Montreal (for Callaghan always an oddly anglophone place), provided him the kind of setting sufficiently metropolitan to enable him to imbue his fictional visions with locality without descending into provincialism. Callaghan, like Raymond Souster in poetry, became in fact a member of that very rare species, the truly regional Toronto writer.

It was also, perhaps, a self-preserving instinct that kept Callaghan in Toronto. In his earlier years he had the kind of encouragement that might have made a rasher young man pull up his roots and head for the deceptively green fields of New York. Not only did Hemingway place his stories in avant garde magazines, but Scott Fitzgerald brought them to the notice of Scribners, the New York house that published his first books. American writers complimented him extravagantly, and he tells with naïve satisfaction in *That Summer in Paris* how Sinclair Lewis said to him, "Flaubert would have loved your work," and how Hemingway told him that "Tolstoy couldn't have done my 'Wedding Dress' story any better."[15] But Callaghan wisely ignored such siren voices and chose, instead of the probability of remaining a minor New York writer, patronized by celebrities, to make his own way in the Canada where in the fullness of time he became a living classic.

If MacLennan was never tempted to experimental writing at any time, Callaghan did for a while take his modest place in the mainstream of North American modernism, writing his early stories and at least his first novel in the laconic style which Hemingway and others had developed; a realist intent found expression in a prose whose sharp and stony clarity seemed to be the counterpart of imagism in verse. But once Callaghan had made his choice to remain in Canada, he developed his own novelistic form and his own approach to language and imagery. His condensed moralist récits of the 1930s are in their own small way genuinely experimental works of fiction. In *Such Is My Beloved*, *More Joy in Heaven*, and *They Shall Inherit the Earth*, he used tight structure and an admirably controlled prose to produce parables that were well suited to his special purpose. Callaghan was as much aware as MacLennan of the problems of his time, but instead of seeing them from a socio-political standpoint, he viewed them as moral problems that challenged accepted religious practices and attitudes rather than fundamental beliefs. He was probably closer in his perceptions at this period to French Catholic radical writers like François Mauriac and Georges Bernanos than he was to the American writers with whom he had associated in his youth. In spite of his proclaimed rejection of metaphorical prose, Callaghan developed in these simple novellas ways of handling both image and symbol that proclaimed him a born writer in a way that MacLennan never was. He started off with a natural feeling for words and the power of sharp visualization that goes with imagist kinds of writing.

But such gifts are not necessarily durable, and the promise Callaghan showed in the 1930s was only partially sustained. Only two of his later books show the degree of artistry and the sureness of tone he developed in the works of the 1930s; these were his memoir, *That Summer in Paris* (1963) and his late novella, *Close to the Sun Again* (1977). The long interval between these books and the works of the 1930s began with a period of virtual silence lasting from 1937 when *More Joy in Heaven* appeared, to 1951 when he published *The Loved and the Lost*. During that long unproductive interlude, whose cause can only be conjectured, the only book of any significance he wrote was the juvenile novel, *Luke Baldwin's Vow* (1948), which until recently has been neglected by the critics.

When Callaghan took up novel writing again at the beginning of the 1950s, his experimental period was clearly at an end. He abandoned the tense, concise form of the 1930s and attempted to write large complex novels that drew to a great extent on the conventions of romance; he failed in that field largely because of the laconism of his dialogue, which was well-suited for short stories or moralist novellas, but seemed gauche and jejune in a more elaborately structured kind of fiction. *The Many Colored Coat* was partly redeemed by its strong ironic element, but both *The Loved and the Lost* and *A Passion in Rome* had more ambition than authenticity, and it was not until Callaghan returned to formal modesty that he was really successful again.

Gary Boire[16] has approached Callaghan selectively rather than comprehensively, and the advantage of this approach is that it saves both the critic and the reader from considering Callaghan's less successful books, though whether picking out the plums is the best critical approach is obviously a matter of debate. Perhaps one cannot object greatly to the fact that Boire gave close attention to only one of Callaghan's early novels, *Strange Fugitive*, and virtually ignored *It's Never Over* and *A Broken Journey*, since these are all apprentice works in which we see Callaghan struggling out from under his early American influences and becoming the real literary self that emerges in the short novels of the 1930s. At this point, however, though *Such Is My Beloved* and *More Joy in Heaven* make a neat pair for purposes of comparison, as Boire has used them, it seems unfortunate that the central piece of the 1930s triptych, *They Shall Inherit the Earth*, is left out, since it is the most complex of the three novels and has a special interest because it shows how closely aware Callaghan was of the social situation in the 1930s, even though he was not one of those who found in political action a viable approach.

Coming to the period of Callaghan's longer novels in the 1950s and 1960s, there is no doubt that in picking *The Many Colored Coat* Boire has chosen the most successful of the three, but one still asks why he did not examine more closely the real failures of the period, *The Loved and the Lost* and *A Passion in Rome*, since it is surely of interest that a writer so sure of his way in the shorter fictional forms, the story and the récit, should have been so much at sea when he embarked on large and intricately planned novels in the conventional manner.

To give attention to *Luke Baldwin's Vow* is enterprising, because the book has up to now received so little attention and is, after all, the only link between the shorter novels of the 1930s and the later longer novels. But one wonders at the elaborate defence Boire presents of *A Fine and Private Place*, which even writers friendly to Callaghan greeted with embarrassment on the author's behalf. In this work of mingled resentment and vanity, Callaghan projects himself in the character of an unappreciated novelist and, none too indirectly, praises himself and damns his critics. Twenty-five years ago Edmund Wilson set a strange hare running when he called Callaghan "the most unjustly neglected novelist in the English-speaking world."[17] That was patently untrue in 1965, and even less true in 1975 when Callaghan published *A Fine and Private Place*, for by then he had received both the Molson Prize and the Royal Bank Award, as near to the Nobel as a Canadian can achieve on his or her own soil.

The case of Callaghan really brings us back to the kind of claims we can make for Canadian writers. Callaghan's flatterers compared him with Tolstoy and Flaubert and sometimes even today one hears these comparisons echoed. But there is no work of his that has the sheer scale of *War and Peace* or *Anna Karenina*, nor did he share Tolstoy's command of the elements of time and place in fiction; and he was never an innovator as original as Flaubert nor did he share his fine and accurate sense of the world. It is like comparing rye whiskey with vodka and armagnac; they are different drinks entirely. And the real question arises: why do we have to make comparisons with writers in other times and places? Every artist's achievement relates first to his or her own time and place, and can be seen best within the setting of his or her own tradition. Sometimes there are foreign influences that are interesting, indeed. Sometimes it is valuable to compare the way in which, say, a Russian writer has rendered the life of the steppes and a Canadian writer the life of the prairie. But these are very specific matters. They are not comparisons of total oeuvres. In terms of final achievement every writer stands on his or her own and must be judged alone. Nobody thinks of comparing Tolstoy with Callaghan. And surely it only belittles Callaghan's special achievement to feel it necessary to compare him with Tolstoy. We are all, in the night of creation as in the night of death, alone.

Howard O'Hagan stands apart from the writers discussed in this section, both in the original mixture of legend and realism he achieved in his single novel *Tay John*, but also in the long neglect he suffered, waiting for a younger generation who would find things to admire in his work and things to borrow. The novel appeared at the beginning of World War II and went largely unrecognized. Though he continued to write stories and hack articles, O'Hagan never produced another work that dragged his novel back into prominence. *Tay John* was not reprinted until 1960. Even now it is not widely recognized except among young West Coast writers who realized how much was to be learned from O'Hagan's tall-telling manner and his larger-than-life characters. In the novel, Tay John, a half-breed Indian who is born in his mother's grave, takes on the dimensions of a messiah for his people, who believe he will lead them to a lost paradise. Instead, after certain prodigious deeds, he disappears into the earth with the body of a pregnant lady traveller. O'Hagan's combination of fantasy, hyperbole, and realism made its appeal to the metafictional generation of the 1970s. Yet critical reception was slow in coming. You will not find a mention of *Tay John* in the 1965 *Literary History of Canada*, and the first real critical essay on O'Hagan was one I published as late as 1974 in *Canadian Literature*. It was by Michael Ondaatje, and the affinities between the two writers were obvious. But it was particularly among Western writers, once his continuing presence among them became known, that O'Hagan became a real influence. Rudy Wiebe, Robert Kroetsch, Robert Harlow, and Jack Hodgins all show the mark of his influence, which closes the gap between the fiction of the 1930s and that of the decades after World War II.

NOTES

[1] *Canadian Writers and Their Works*, ed. Robert Lecker, Jack David, and Ellen Quigley, Fiction ser., v (Toronto: ECW, 1990), pp. 79, 149; hereafter cited as *CWTW*.

[2] *CWTW*, Fiction ser., v, p. 234.

[3] Desmond Pacey, rev. of *At the Tide's Turn and Other Stories*, by Thomas H. Raddall; *Arcadian Adventures with the Idle Rich*, by Stephen Leacock; *Habitant Poems*, by W.H. Drummond; and *Poets of the Confederation*, ed. Malcolm Ross, *Queen's Quarterly*, 68 (1961), 180.

[4] George Woodcock, "Raddall: The Making of the Story-teller," *Saturday Night*, Nov. 1976, p. 69.

[5] John Moss, *A Reader's Guide to the Canadian Novel* (Toronto: McClelland and Stewart, 1981), p. 230.

[6] D.O. Spettigue, "The Way It Was: Ernest Buckler," in *The Canadian Novel in the Twentieth Century: Essays from* Canadian Literature, New Canadian Library, No. 115, ed. George Woodcock (Toronto: McClelland and Stewart, 1975), p. 147.

[7] Spettigue, p. 155.

[8] Alan R. Young, "The Genesis of Ernest Buckler's *The Mountain and the Valley*," in *Modern Times*, Vol. III of *The Canadian Novel: A Critical Anthology*, ed. John Moss (Toronto: NC, 1982), pp. 195–205.

[9] W.J. Keith, *Canadian Literature in English* (London: Longman, 1985), p. 148.

[10] *CWTW*, Fiction ser., v, p. 40.

[11] Keith, p. 148.

[12] Morley Callaghan, *That Summer in Paris: Memories of Tangled Friendships with Hemingway, Fitzgerald, and Some Others* (Toronto: Macmillan, 1963), p. 22.

[13] Elspeth Cameron, "Of Cabbages and Kings: The Concept of Hero in *The Watch That Ends the Night*," in *Modern Times*, Vol. III of *The Canadian Novel: A Critical Anthology*, ed. John Moss (Toronto: NC, 1982), pp. 126–27.

[14] *CWTW*, Fiction ser., V, p. 155.

[15] Callaghan, pp. 69, 38.

[16] *CWTW*, Fiction ser., V, p. 98.

[17] Edmund Wilson, "Morley Callaghan of Toronto," in *O Canada: An American's Notes on Canadian Culture* (New York: Farrar, Straus and Giroux, 1965), p. 9.

CHAPTER 6

All Kinds to Make a World:
Ethel Wilson, Mordecai Richler,
Robertson Davies, Hugh Garner,
Adele Wiseman

INEVITABLY, in making a selection of essays like the present series, which aims to discuss critically the most important of a country's writers, the attempt to arrange groups by affinity must occasionally break down. One sometimes encounters a cluster of novelists who belong roughly to the same period, but otherwise seem to exemplify nothing more felicitously than the old saying that it takes all kinds to make a world. But in a literary world, variegation is a sign of aesthetic maturity, an earnest of escaping the tyranny of labels, whether colonialist or nationalist, and of spreading out into the open parkland of the free intelligence, the unconstrained sensibility.

The five writers herein are certainly varied; they share neither generation nor social or educational background. Ethel Wilson was born forty-three years before Mordecai Richler, and twenty-five years before her nearest contemporaries, Robertson Davies and Hugh Garner. An important part of her life was lived in a late-Victorian and Edwardian setting unknown, except through read-ing, by any of the writers here associated with her; her store of experience, her view of the world, her morality, and even the kind of prose she wrote were all affected by this privileged primacy.

Ethel Wilson and Robertson Davies both came from what George Orwell, himself a member of it, used to call the "lower upper middle class." Their educations at such institutions of their caste as Miss Gordon's School (later the patrician Crofton House School) and Upper Canada College shaped their initial outlooks; the extraordinary thing about Wilson was that in the end she came to empathize so well with poor and unlettered people, like Mort and Myrt in "Tuesday and Wednesday" and the "pale slut" Lilly, who so remarkably remakes herself in the companion novella, "Lilly's Story." Hugh Garner, on the other hand, came from the farthest side of the tracks; he was an authentic example, by origin at least, of that rare species so carefully sought in the 1930s and so rarely found, the real proletarian writer. Finally, Adele Wiseman, reared in Winnipeg, and Mordecai Richler, brought up in Montreal, shared an area of experience unknown to the others, since they grew up in half-assimilated Jewish families who still lived in immigrant urban areas that were not very far from being ghettos.

Perhaps what most unites this group of five notable but dissimilar novelists is their relative literary conservatism, their shared lack of interest in literary experimentation on any more enterprising level than Richler's Swiftian satiric grotesqueries. In writing of Davies, John Mills talks of the ferment that had been going on in twentieth-century literature ever since Henry James, and he adds:

> None of this ferment seems to have affected Robertson Davies. Though he uses Jungian concepts to structure his fictional characters, his novels are conventional in form and genre. . . . Davies clearly belongs to a reactionary camp in these matters, but it is as though formalism and the general question of "form" hold no interest for him and that what he has to say can best be said only in the traditional manner.[1]

Wilson, too, tended to find her models outside the Americas and largely outside the twentieth century, and though she denied any awareness of having been influenced by any other writer, she once picked out Defoe, Fielding, Trollope, Proust, Forster, and Ivy Compton-Burnett as special favourites, and really defined herself as a writer in what it seemed to her they had in common:

> . . . I would say that the limpid style of most of them, the lack of pretentiousness, the fact that these people have something to say, with skill, with good heart, often with deep feeling yet with some cynicism, their detachment as well as their involvement, gives one inexpressible pleasure. They have *style*, each his own, and without style . . . how dull.[2]

83

Clearly if Davies has — and I think Mills is correct in this — no really deep interest in form, seeking rather with a craftsman's skill the most convenient frame for whatever bizarre human situation his imagination might throw up, form — even when she called it *style* — meant a great deal to Wilson. In fact, she was a fine and subtle formalist. So, at his very best in a few short stories, was Hugh Garner, though such epiphanies rarely came to him.

If Wilson never cut her European roots, and Davies equally retained them, such novelists nevertheless wrote in a quite different setting from those earlier Canadian writers whose problem was how to escape from colonial imitativeness. Their task was not that of Roberts and Lampman and D.C. Scott — how to regenerate a vitiated late-Romantic English literary technique by relating it to Canadian experience. It was, rather, how to relate the literature of an emergent Canadian nation to a world setting in which the traditional and the modern had come together in an extraordinary flowering, manifested in such different ways by James and Eliot and Proust.

Naïve nationalists have tended to see the solution in Little Canadianism, in virtually asserting that here, in our brief traditions and experience, we have enough to produce a literature and a culture of our own, and, in consequence, in virtually turning their backs on all the glories and all the resources of world literature. None of the writers discussed in these essays came to such a foolish conclusion, yet at the same time none was under the illusion that there was any way in which the experience of living in Canada could be denied as the essential content of Canadian writing, a content that — as contents always do — must reshape the form. And so, while we see Wilson and Davies seeking their mentors in the art of writing among their English predecessors and contemporaries, and Garner and Richler among the American fictional realists of the era between the great wars, and Wiseman largely turning back to the Yiddish traditions we associate not only with Sholom Aleichem but with that magical and too-forgotten writer, Mendele Mocher Sforim, what they write belongs to the Canadian experience in a way the works of nineteenth-century colonialist writers did not, because, no matter how much they sometimes tried — as Richler especially did — they could not escape from the land that made them.

Conversely, in the vision of Canada that we have acquired in the late twentieth century, the données of such writers shape our view of Canadian society, as the paintings of the Group of Seven shape our way of seeing the Canadian landscape. And out of such perceptions, filtered from the great world tradition through our own writers, emerged the phenomenon we call Canadian literature. I find myself quoted in one of these essays as asserting in 1973 that ". . . a Pacific literary sensibility . . . began to come into being when Ethel Wilson published her novels about the Coast . . ."[3] and I stand by what I said.

Ethel Wilson's writing was greatly influenced, I believe, by her own peculiar literary biography. She was born in 1888, which made her just three years younger than D.H. Lawrence and six years older than Aldous Huxley and J.B. Priestley; as a child, she had known Arnold Bennett, whom she once defended because of his feeling for poor people against Virginia Woolf's strictures. Yet, starting to write extraordinarily late, she did not publish her first short story until 1937, when she was forty-nine, and *Hetty Dorval*, her first novel, appeared in 1947, when she was fifty-nine, six years older than Mordecai Richler is now, at — and perhaps over — the peak of his literary trajectory. Her career, after that, was remarkably short, for the last of her six books, *Mrs. Golightly and Other Stories*, appeared in 1961, and the last of her contributions to literary periodicals, in 1964. Though she lived until 1980, she withdrew in her later years into the silence of sickness and bereavement. Thus her whole career as a writer lasted for only twenty-seven out of her ninety-two years, and her books all appeared within an even briefer period of fourteen years.

I consider that in this temporal disjunction between experience and creation lie many of the clues to the special character of Wilson's writing. In another piece written a decade ago which remembered my friendship with her, I remarked that "she had retained, I realized, an Edwardian sensibility, but she had developed a contemporary ironic intelligence, and it was the interplay of the two that gave her books their special quality."[4] The Edwardian sensibility is most in evidence in that moving, and at the same time very amusing, chronicle of an eccentric English-woman transplanted to Victorian Vancouver, *The Innocent Traveller*, and the contemporary ironic intelligence certainly inspires the first and last of her important novels, *Hetty Dorval* and *Swamp Angel*.

At one point in an essay on Wilson, Beverley Mitchell remarks that ". . . she reveals the qualities which F.R. Leavis considered characteristic of writers in the 'great tradition': 'a vital capacity for experience, a . . . reverent openness before life, and a marked moral intensity.' "[5] Those qualities are all there indeed, and Wilson was certainly aware of a great tradition and her adherence to it. She distrusted fads in literature, and she was just as unhappy about fads in criticism (though she valued the critical function), and though she used symbolism sparingly but skilfully, she was especially perturbed by any broadly symbolic interpretation of her work. Her great virtue indeed lies in her power to record experience, not literally, but faithfully, and it is out of this recording and out of her remarkably clear observation of people and places that her symbolism and the formal structure of her novels emerge by natural extension; one never has the feeling that any symbol appearing in her books is deliberately invented, either for its own sake or to evade the difficulties of clear and direct expression.

I talk about the "clear observation of people and places," and in that phrase, it seems to me, is contained the dual pattern that gives so much of its interest to Wilson's work. For she presents the combination — unusual anywhere and especially in Canada — of the novelist of manners and the novelist concerned in a lyrical way with the natural world and man's place in it. She is greatly interested in the details of daily life and the modes of human behaviour and intercourse, and in representing them she has something of the wit and playfulness of a Peacock as well as the wry understanding of a Jane Austen. She is especially interested in the human power of self-deception, and Mitchell rightly stresses the role of the "unreliable narrator" in *Hetty Dorval*.

Yet, at the same time, Wilson was so intensely open to the appeal of natural setting, of the places she and her characters inhabit, that she writes of them with a shimmering intensity that reminds one of the young D.H. Lawrence. She valued Proust especially for his concern with place, from which, she once said, "he took his text," and she herself certainly took her text from the place she lived in. She said as much in the 1960 essay "The Bridge or the Stokehold?: Views of the Novelist's Art":

But in retrospect I see my Canadianness, for example, in that my locale in a sustained piece of writing (that is, in a book) has to be British Columbia. There are other places in the world that I know and love, but none that I know, and feel, and love in the same way. But I did not choose it. It chose. It is very strong.[6]

Indeed, Ethel Wilson's few books, brief as they are intense, have their unchallengeable place in the record of Canadian fiction most of all because they represented the first successful attempt to bring the physical setting of Western Canada convincingly into fiction, so that their comedies of manners and their dramas of feeling are played out against superbly realized backdrops of landscape.

Robertson Davies, on the other hand, has almost no sense of place; and, whether in his Salterton or his Deptford novels, descriptions of towns are slight and hardly necessary to the narrative, and evocations of landscape are almost nonexistent. His early interest in theatre, his brief career as an actor, and his not unsuccessful career as a dramatist should prepare one for the relatively narrow world of his novels, where "all the world's a stage" is to be understood in its most reductive sense, with the world narrowed down to the places where people encounter each other. His novels are almost as dramatic as Peacock's or Meredith's, depending for their effect on the verbal encounters of the characters and on the kind of grand acting and theatrical machinery that fill his later books with a great deal of amusing, and some sinister, humbug.

Wilson wrote close to life. Davies, though he often writes like a realist, in a straightforward colloquial prose, always does so at a remove, as though he were looking across the footlights. Everything he writes is in one way or another satirical, and satire is a safe distance to keep. In the Deptford novels especially — *Fifth Business*, *The Manticore*, and *World of Wonders* — he drifts often into fantasy situations, Jungian and otherwise, creating larger-than-life characters who sometimes have the bogus papier-mâché feel of carnival figures, dabbling in conjury rather than magic, and amusing himself with introducing a rather theatrically contrived evil into quiet corners of life that seem obvious boltholes for the nervous. All this has led the academic critics into some highfalutin symbolic and allegorical interpretations, in which Davies has obviously gloried even when he has wisely refused to commit himself to any of them. It has also, less surprisingly in this era addicted to neo-Gothicism, turned him into what John Mills calls "a best-selling, mid-cult novelist."[7]

Much of this double success is due to the prose which Mills at various times calls "effortless" and "glib," and this in turn is related to another facet of Davies' multi-talented persona, his role as a man of letters, ready to turn his hand to any kind of respectable prose, and ultimately concerned to teach as much as to delight, a concern that led him into the academic world and kept him there long enough to write *The Rebel Angels*, one of the few interesting novels written about Canadian universities. The didactic editor of the *Peterborough Examiner* and the Master of Massey College are not remarkably far apart at the two ends of a brilliant career, and the novels can be seen as spanning the space between.

John Mills clearly prefers Davies' early novels to his later, more ambitious, and more popular books. His reasoning here may be less than impeccable for he declares that "*Tempest-Tost, Leaven of Malice*, and *A Mixture of Frailties* are generally more successful books than their less conventional successors since their genesis lies more in the desire to entertain than to instruct."[8] But surely, in critical terms, the distinction between entertainment and instruction is subordinate to a judgement of the aesthetic success or failure of the work, and however much entertainment and instruction may enter into the final synthesis of the work, we do not — if we consider it seriously — consider first of all whether it is good fun or teaches a salutary lesson.

However, the criterion Mills uses is in a special way justified when dealing with Davies since the combination of entertainer and instructor is particularly striking in his case, and perhaps more than anything else it determines the shape of his literary persona. And I am ready to grant that the fact of his handling entertainment more neatly than instruction does, in different ways, affect the ultimate success of the works in both periods. Davies does produce well-made novels in which his prose rings clearly and the play of manners is carried on with a skill that is so closely related to Davies' concurrent success as a dramatist that it is unfortunate Mills allowed the fact that he had not seen the plays to prevent him from discussing them in relation to the novels. They are perhaps lesser works, in literary terms at least, but necessary for a full understanding of his whole career as a writer.

The Deptford novels, as I see them, belong in the category of imperfect works which, if they are not great, border on grandeur, not so much in the sense of Frederick Philip Grove's inspired awkwardness, but rather in the Dickensian sense, for thinking of the Davies of this period I am reminded of what Orwell said of Dickens — that he "is obviously a writer whose parts are greater than his wholes. He is all fragments, all details — rotten architecture, but wonderful gargoyles. . . ."9 In the Deptford novels, the parts do indeed distract us from the whole, so that we become preoccupied with the extraordinary play of coincidence and its highlighting of bizarre incidents, rather than with the development of character, which in these novels — as Mills remarks — is "lacking in sharp focus," or even with the precision of instruction. For what, after all Davies' effort and ours, have we learned didactically from the Deptford novels, apart from some lessons about individuation we might have understood better from a direct reading of Jung, and some quasi-existentialist reflections on the nature of destiny and the internal forces that shape it that have been handled by writers like Albert Camus with a great deal less pretentious mumbo-jumbo than that which makes *World of Wonders* such an interesting read and in the end such a disappointing novel? Here a word should be said for *The Rebel Angels*, which with its successors seems a tacit recognition on his part of the flaws of his more pretentious period. By returning to the academic ambiance of the Salterton novels, he has once again contained the action within a picture stage, yet by *exploiting* the stage's limitations he has been able to turn to effective satiric use the grotesqueries of character and action that he so often seemed to develop without purpose in the Deptford novels.

Robertson Davies and Hugh Garner may have had more in common than either would have cared to admit. At first sight, they seem diametrical opposites. Davies, by upbringing and inclination, is a pillar of the establishment, collecting doctorates and other honours almost as assiduously as Northrop Frye. His values are gentlemanly, and his behaviour, one gathers, has been the same. Garner received only one honour in his life, a Governor-General's Award, and made the occasion an opportunity to show his contempt for authority when, after Roland Michener had recited the citation, he broke the awed silence of Rideau Hall with his loud and gravelly voice, asking: "Have you read it?"[10] He was hardly, as those will remember who suffered him in his moods of drunken aggression, a gentleman in any usually accepted sense of the word. And, indeed, he took a constant pride in being a loner, at odds with the world, in general, and even more at odds with the literary world. He kept himself so much apart from the tribe that few other writers knew him well.

What he did have in common with Davies was the craftsmanly dedication that made it a matter of pride with him to be able to write acceptably in any context. When Davies did this, he was referred to as a man of letters, but when Garner did it, he was more likely to be dismissed as a hack, and there was at least some justification in this, as any one who reads even a selected volume like *Hugh Garner's Best Stories* (the book that won him the Governor-General's Award) will appreciate, for he could always cut his coat to his cloth and gave popular magazines what they wanted in style and even in length.

If Garner was a hack, it was in the Defoe tradition, for whenever he had the opportunity, he wrote with an artistry that often reached a high level, and the best of his stories, which he hoped would bring him "a little bit of immortality,"[11] justly have their regular places in Canadian anthologies; even in his less pretentious stories for slick magazines, he was, as Paul Stuewe remarks, "exhibiting his professionalism and craftsmanship at the same time as he [was] publishing work that has little to do with literature."[12]

I talked of Garner at the beginning of this chapter as a rare example of the "real proletarian writer," and one of his most interesting aspects is that, almost alone in Canada, he has written a fiction clearly based on class. His best-known and best novel, *Cabbagetown,* is not merely an interesting piece of realistic fiction; it is also a remarkable study of the way working people lived in Toronto not long ago, a study supplemented by what Garner tells us about his own slum youth in his autobiography, *One Damn Thing after Another.* In books like these, we find Garner's true traditions coming together. For his stylistic masters were the American realists of the early part of the century, and especially John Dos Passos, who, he said, taught him "how realistic fiction should be written."[13] But the attitude that inspires the content in his novels is English to the core; no Canadian writer has quite so thoroughly projected the passions that inspire the English class system at all its levels, or has written so much about the pride that a true working man takes in the actual *work* that gives him his place in society, his class. One can, without exaggeration, see in the pride that Garner took in a writing task well done a projection of the old-fashioned working man's pride that valued such virtues as decency and cleanliness as much as any bourgeois.

All this is remote from the fictional preoccupations of Ethel Wilson and Robertson Davies. It is true that Garner, like Wilson, had a sense of place, but it is urban place, and, even more, work place; when he does write on rural subjects, he sets with brilliant clarity the immediate situation in which, say, tobacco pickers do their work on a southern Ontario farm, but the countryside in itself hardly exists for him.

Garner saw his work as existing within the realist tradition. But, apart from the strength of his class passions, there was a great deal of sentimental feeling in his books, and his realism was certainly of the moralistic kind. He was never at any point in his career a fashionable writer, and he made himself felt by the harsh independence of his attitude and by the fact that his writing was never less than workmanlike and often a great deal better, so that he maintained both a popular paperback following and the respect of many fellow novelists, even if the critics gave him less than his due. He is likely to have his place in literary memoirs as an eccentric personality, but it would be unfortunate if he were remembered merely as a falling-down-drunk writer, which sometimes he was. *Cabbagetown* is a fine example of the social novel, one of the best ever produced in Canada, and a dozen or so of his stories are likely to assure him a lasting place in Canadian fiction. Yet he still stands, after his death, as an inveterately solitary individual, with no close literary kindred, a writer self-taught and self-sustained in every sense of the phrase, and in his own way an admirable example of artistic dedication.

Garner fought in the Spanish civil war during the 1930s as a member of the International Brigades, but, curiously enough, the experience had less direct influence on his writing than the myth of Spain, as it became by the 1940s, had on the writing of Mordecai

Richler. All three writers I have so far discussed began to write and publish before World War II: Richler, like Adele Wiseman, began to write some time after the end of the war, during the years that were overshadowed by the buildup of the Cold War on a world stage and of the McCarthy terror in the United States, and one of the most persistent elements in his novels has been his ambiguous relationship to the old left of the 1930s and afterwards.

There are, in fact, three poles of place in Richler's writings. One is Spain, which — notably in his first novel, *The Acrobats*, but even to some extent in his later, *Joshua Then and Now* — arouses in him a kind of dark romanticism verging on the Gothic: Spain as the home of lost causes, where their destroyers also lurk, personified by the former Nazis who play stage villain's roles in each of these two novels.

The second pole is England, where Richler lived for two decades and wrote most of his fiction, yet which he continued to see with expatriate's eyes, so that it became merely the setting where exiles from North American ghettos and fugitives from North American persecutions lived out a marginal life; in such conditions conducive to alienation, they developed into the kind of hollow men who are subjected to the black humour of Richler's extreme fantasy novel, *Cocksure*. But outside these alien circles, England hardly exists in Richler's novels in any recognizable form. His incomprehension of British society, which Garner would have instinctively understood if he had chosen to live there, is almost as evident as his misreading of Spain, which again is the Spain Richler knew as a wandering young writer mingling with the foreigners on Ibiza and whose image betrays an almost complete failure to empathize with the Spaniards themselves, their culture, or their history.

Of course, one does not expect a novel to be a travel book, revealing the scenery and life-styles of a strange land to its reader. Fiction, in so far as it is not gratuitous invention, is a distillation of subjective experience, rather than an objective reportage. But the way a writer portrays the settings in which he has lived does help us understand the character of his work and his perceptions. And the fact that Richler's perceptions of Montreal, and especially of its Jewish society and the physical environment of Saint Urbain Street, are authentic as well as movingly expressed, not only shows us his real roots, but also tells us what kind of a novelist he is.

First of all, it tells us that, though Richler struggled hard against the Canadian literary nationalism of the 1960s, and though, as Kerry McSweeney rightly remarks, "It was America, not Canada, that provided the young Mordecai Richler with a usable literary tradition and a dynamic modernist milieu . . . ,"[14] the only content in his works that is convincing is in some way Canadian, and the only milieu that has, for better or worse, fed his imagination is that in which he grew up — the Jewish world of Montreal in the 1930s and '40s. "The first twenty years are the most important . . . ," he once said. "After that, certain doors on experience close." And he also said: "I'm a big city Canadian — an urban Jew. . . [I] write out of my Canadian experience, and always will . . . ."[15] This was said in 1969, when he was still living in England and had not finally decided on the return to Montreal he made in 1972.

In this situation, one can see the roots of the virtues and the weaknesses alike of Richler's novels. André Gide once described himself as a novelist without the gift of invention, which, he insisted, did not mean that he was a novelist without imagination. It meant that, however he might adapt it and change its content, Gide was always writing out of his own life and ambiance, rather than inventing new and wholly fictional worlds. One can, reasonably, divide novelists into the inventors and the well-diggers. If the wells are deep enough, there is no doubt they can produce fine novels, when experience has been subjected to all the tricks that memory and artifice can play; Proust is there as the splendid witness. On the other hand, the well-diggers are seldom capable of creating the new worlds, seemingly detached from their own lives, that the inventors can offer. The difference is of kind, not of quality. How can one compare a book straight from the well like *Sons and Lovers* with an invention like *La Chartreuse de Parme*? Or, to bring the question nearer our present subject, Richler's *Bildungsroman*, *Son of a Smaller Hero*, with Matt Cohen's *The Sweet Second Summer of Kitty Malone*?

Though he is a passing good embroiderer of actuality, Richler is not one of the inventors. Everything he writes is drawn from a well sunk somewhere between Mount Royal and the north bank of the Saint Lawrence, and, like the works of other well-diggers, his novels over the years tend to suffer from a monotony of attitude and arrangement, so that nothing he has written since has shown quite the same insolent verve and vigour as his fourth novel, and his second book set in Jewish Montreal, *The Apprenticeship of Duddy Kravitz*, which, it is now a little hard to remember, was published in 1959, when he was twenty-eight, less than halfway through his life up to the present.

For thirty years now, Richler has been dealing in a series of novels, more widely spaced as time goes on, with the same settings (Montreal, London, Spain), the same kind of people (Saint Urbain Jews, expatriate hacks, comic WASPs), the same kind of themes, the same kind of personal relationships, even the same kind of bawdy jokes from the high school john. And while, as musicians and mathematicians know, there is theoretically no reason why an infinitude of variations should not be played on the same theme, in practice the human mind is intolerant of sameness, and readers tend to tire of such repetitions on a well-digger's part, as they do not of the new worlds offered by the inventors. Perhaps this is because writers also tire of too much sameness in their material, as one realizes from reading Richler's *Joshua Then and Now*, the product of waiting nine years for an often-used well to fill.

Kerry McSweeney has followed Richler's novels in the sequence of publication, but it is also helpful to look backward, for any reader familiar with Richler's earlier novels is struck with an acute and not entirely comfortable sense of *déjà vu* on reading *Joshua Then and Now*. And, indeed, we have been here before, more than once. The situation, as in *St. Urbain's Horseman*, is that of an uncouth, but good-hearted, Montreal Jewish intellectual (a bit of a hack, rather money-grubbing, but in some obscure way honest), married to a long-legged *goyische* beauty. The passionately monogamous marriage — virtuously contrasted with more modish but less harmonious relationships — is threatened by a dire event manipulated from outside by some appalling, faceless *deus ex machina*. In *St. Urbain's Horseman*, it was Jake Hersh's reluctant involvement in an orgy that led to a rape-and-sodomy case, and in *Joshua Then and Now* it is the presumed suicide of Joshua Shapiro's gentile brother-in-law that sends his wife, Pauline, into a nervous breakdown and in turn involves the desperate Joshua in a near-fatal car crash. But in *Joshua*, as in *Horseman*, hero and heroine emerge from the shadows, and all is made well in one of those happy endings in which Richler so often proves the maxim that cynicism always masks a sentimentalist.

Other elements from past novels are built into the ramshackle architecture of *Joshua Then and Now*. Though Joshua now lives in Westmount, his roots are still in the Saint Urbain street ghetto (a ghetto of the mind) of *Son of a Smaller Hero* and *The Apprenticeship of Duddy Kravitz*. The ex-Nazi villain who appeared as Colonel Kraus in Richler's first novel, *The Acrobats*, as Ernst in *A Choice of Enemies*, and as the elusive Dr. Mengele in *St. Urbain's Horseman*, is here again in the crazy Dr. Dr. Mueller, whom Joshua as a young man encounters on Ibiza (itself a flashback). Dr. Dr. Mueller becomes the object of an obsessive quest by middle-aged Joshua just as Dr. Mengele was the object of an equally bizarre quest by Jake Hersh and (in Jake's fantasy) by his elusive cousin Joey Hersh, alias de la Hirsch, the horseman of Saint Urbain.

Joshua Then and Now is built up in a series of random flashbacks from the point where Joshua is in his Lake Memphremagog home, convalescing from his accident and wondering about his temporarily vanished wife. But the past is less skilfully manipulated than in *St. Urbain's Horseman*. In more than four hundred pages, we are told how Joshua got into his scrape, as the narrative wanders, sometimes with little evident purpose, through the labyrinths of his past — and Richler's past novels — Montreal, London, Ibiza. It has the hasty disorder of a collage, rather than the coherence of a mosaic; one wonders what Richler did in all those nine years of rewriting and polishing to produce so roughly built a book in the end.

Yet Richler still had the skill that prevents him from falling for long into the pretentious dullness — Grove's Disease — that afflicts so much Canadian fiction. His prose varies between the extravagant and the toughly flat, and does not often sink into the looseness that imperils the general structure of *Joshua Then and Now*. As Joshua thinks of the seventh novel of his friend Murdoch, Richler's eighth novel is — with all its faults — "written with a fine writer's remembered skills." If, remembering his prose skills, Richler had only forgotten his plots, everything would have been more interesting. Clearly he had reached the point when only a major shift of direction can revivify his work.

That shift seemed to become evident when *Solomon Gursky Was Here*, arguably Richler's best novel, appeared in 1989. It was a kind of satiric panorama of the great originative myths of Canadian history, exploration, and trade. The sporadic narrator, Moses Berger, son of a Montreal Jewish poet and himself a drunken writer, fulfills a similar role to Jake Hersh in *St. Urbain's Horseman*, for he is obsessed with the fate of Solomon Gursky, a maverick son of a rich Jewish family that made its fortune out of bootlegging in the days of Prohibition and is descended from a Jewish petty crook who escaped from the penal settlements of Australia to join the Franklin expedition as surgeon's assistant. Taking ample supplies of kosher food on board, Ephraim Gursky escapes the lead poisoning that kills off the rest of the crew, and survives as a kind of shaman among the Inuit until he finally comes south to Lower Canada, establishing there a Church of the Millenarians, and starting the business that with his grandsons becomes a prosperous and respectable firm of distillers.

It reads like a *roman à clef*, and though Richler asserts that "I invented the Gurskys out of my own head," most Canadian readers will turn their key in the same way and come up with the same family in real life. But in fictional terms the main interest of the novel lies in its central similarity to *St. Urbain's Horseman*, for like the protagonist of that novel, Moses Berger is seeking a lost man whom he fantasizes into a hero. The point of both books is the question of the absent central figure, who never appears in the present of the novel, at least under his own name. Solomon Gursky remains a dream that haunts all those who have known him — and even some like Moses who have not — and his insubstantiality is complemented by the very substantiality of the rest of the novel which recreates the world Richler once knew, a lost anglophone Montreal seen from the ghetto of St. Urbain.

Solomon Gursky Was Here seems to reconcile the two manners that were in conflict or at least in competition in Richler's early writings — the fantastic and the realistic. In the vividly remembered Montreal life (especially in *Son of a Smaller Hero* and *The Apprenticeship of Duddy Kravitz*) it is realism (not naturalism) that prevails, heavily tempered with satire. In the foreign scenes, the tendency is for the satire to switch to fantasy, creating grotesque and implausible hollow figures, beginning with Kraus, the unlikely Nazi of *The Acrobats*, and reaching an apogee in the Starmaker, the monstrous gangster-tycoon of *Cocksure*. In *St. Urbain's Horse-*

man and *Solomon Gursky Was Here* the fantasy indeed persists, as Joey the Horseman and Solomon Gursky are presented going out on their unlikely quests, but what the novels mainly explore is the fantastic nature of what goes on in the actual world, particularly seen through the eyes of a stranger.

For Richler is still the exile, the essential Canadian, unable to render except in caricature anything outside that hypnotic circle of locality which creates what Northrop Frye called "the garrison mentality." What his novels suggest is that "the idea of a Jew" is very much like the idea of a Canadian, for Canada is a land of minorities, regions, disguised ghettos. In that lies Richler's appeal to his countrymen, and the reason why he is never considered as other than a Canadian writer.

Adele Wiseman differs from the four other novelists I have been discussing in that she has not felt in any way the need for continuous production that made Richler and Garner and Davies into professional writers even in the economic sense, and led Wilson, who was spurred by no economic imperatives, to write continuously during the period when she was an active writer. Wiseman barely avoids being classified as a one-book writer. She published the book by which she is justly best known, *The Sacrifice*, in 1956. Her only other novel, *Crackpot*, appeared in 1974. A slight memoir on her mother, *Old Woman at Play*, an equally slight book on immigrant markets, a short story, and two plays, one published privately, seem to complete her entire visible literary production over twenty-eight years.

As will be evident, her work, except for the two novels, has consisted of *divertissements*, and even the second novel, *Crackpot*, is a flawed exuberant book, the fictional biography of an innocent whore, which, for all the indulgence Wiseman expends on her wayward antiheroine, has too much of the *fausse naïve* in the composition of its character to be really convincing. It is interesting mainly as an offshoot of the Polish-Yiddish picaresque tradition represented by such nineteenth-century works as Mendele Mocher Sforim's *Fishke the Lame*.

The Yiddish fictional tradition is also evident in *The Sacrifice*, Wiseman's major novel, but only as one element, for *The Sacrifice* is also, as John Moss has said, "an example of immigrant fiction . . . without peer."[16] Wiseman in *The Sacrifice* goes deeper, in terms of Jewish tradition, than Richler, who is concerned mainly with the half-assimilated second generation putting down stronger roots in the new land than its fathers. Nor is she concerned merely with the immigrant experience. She is involved also with the pogrom experience, which made Jews from the Holy Russian Empire into refugees and hence immigrants. So *The Sacrifice* has a basis in history and tradition deeper than most other Canadian Jewish writing. But beyond that, it reaches down into myth, the myth of the original Abraham and his angelic deliverance from the duty to sacrifice, a deliverance no longer available to his modern successor, a wanderer in the New World as his namesake was in the Old, Abraham the crazed killer who emerged from Wiseman's imagination. This, indeed, is more than an immigrant novel; it is a novel about how, entering promised Canaan, the pilgrim still has to come to terms with his past in the land of Egypt. Here, I think, John Moss's gloss admirably complements Michael Greenstein's careful analysis:

> The pattern of loss, isolation, struggle, and assimilation that marks the genre [immigrant fiction] is here rendered with authenticity and dramatic intensity that makes all other such novels seem pale imitations. Perhaps because immigrant experience is not an end in itself, but the supporting structure upon which Wiseman builds a complex allegory of spiritual duress, the immigrant in this novel is universal, both an everyman and (as his name, Abraham, implies) our common source.[17]

In Canada we are all immigrants. Wherever Man first appeared — mythologically in the Mesopotamian Garden of Eden or biologically in the development of equivocally named Homo sapiens and his displacement of that large-brain Neanderthaler whose potentialities were never tested — it was certainly nowhere in the Americas. There are no autochthonous Canadians, even among the Indians and the Inuit. And so a book so powerful in its evocation of the universal trauma of coming as a stranger into a new land as *The Sacrifice*, is likely to have a lasting place in our literature.

NOTES

1 *Canadian Writers and Their Works*, ed. Robert Lecker, Jack David, and Ellen Quigley, Fiction ser., VI (Toronto: ECW, 1985), p. 23; hereafter cited as *CWTW*.

2 Quoted in Desmond Pacey *Ethel Wilson*, Twayne's World Authors Series, No. 33 (New York: Twayne, 1967), p. 18.

3 George Woodcock, "Getting Away from Us All," *Maclean's*, June 1973, p. 96.

4 George Woodcock, "Ethel Wilson," *Canadian Fiction Magazine*, No. 15 (Autumn 1974), pp. 44–49; rpt. in *The World of Canadian Writing: Critiques and Recollections*, by George Woodcock (Vancouver: Douglas & McIntyre, 1980), p. 122.

5 F.R. Lewis, *The Great Tradition: George Eliot, Henry James, Joseph Conrad* (London: Chatto and Windus, 1973), p. 9.

6 *Canadian Literature*, No. 5 (Summer 1960), p. 44.

7 *CWTW*, Fiction ser., VI, p. 69

8 *CWTW*, Fiction ser., VI, p. 33.

9 George Orwell, *An Age like This: 1920–1940*, Vol. 1 of *The Collected Essays, Journalism and Letters of George Orwell*, ed. Sonia Orwell and Ian Angus (New York: Harcourt, Brace & World, 1968), p. 454.

10 I had this from Roy Daniells, an eyewitness of the occasion.

11 Allan Anderson, "An Interview with Hugh Garner," *The Tamarack Review*, No. 52 (1969), pp. 29–30.

12 *CWTW*, Fiction ser., VI, p. 112.

13 Hugh Garner, *One Damn Thing After Another* (Toronto: McGraw-Hill Ryerson, 1973), p. 20.

14 *CWTW*, Fiction ser., VI, p. 135.

15 Quoted in George Woodcock, *Mordecai Richler*, New Canadian Library, Canadian Writers Series, No. 6 (Toronto: McClelland and Stewart, 1971), p. 4.

16 John Moss, *A Reader's Guide to the Canadian Novel* (Toronto: McClelland and Stewart, 1981), p. 288.

17 Moss, p. 288.

CHAPTER 7

One's Own Vision and Experience:
Clark Blaise, Hugh Hood,
John Metcalf, Alice Munro,
Sheila Watson

WRITING ON ALICE MUNRO, Hallvard Dahlie seems to set the keynote for one's reading of the whole cluster of writers here represented when he remarks,

> Alice Munro occupies a solid position in that group of writers whose careers coincided with the artistic, cultural, and political coming-of-age of Canada after World War II, a period during which the intrinsic value of Canadian experience came to be taken for granted. Unlike those writers who attained their maturity between the two world wars, or who were conditioned by Old World attitudes, sentiments, and values, this younger group felt no obligation or compulsion to see their world in any other terms than those defined by their own vision and experience.[1]

If there is a sense in which these writers do move beyond "their own vision and experience," it is to be found in the fact that they represent the coming into Canadian fiction, during the 1950s and subsequent decades, of the tradition of modernism, a tradition that had already begun to influence Canadian poetry at least two decades earlier, in the 1930s. And here there is another appropriate quotation, from Stephen Scobie writing on Sheila Watson:

> To speak of Watson's "tradition and milieu" is, in effect, to speak of the whole culture of modernism, which was obsessed

equally by the impulse to order and by the desire, in Ezra Pound's phrase, to "make it new." It was in some ways a very conservative culture, looking back to all-encompassing world views, steeped in the literature and mythology of previous ages; yet, for its contemporaries, it was also revolutionary, an avant-garde, the latest thing.[2]

What most strikingly characterized modernism was the fact that, although its practitioners were not without strong views on politics, religion, and morality, they were concerned, first of all, and in an especially austere way, with aesthetic values and their renewal. In so far as they were writers, Saint John the Evangelist could be taken as their patron saint: "In the beginning was the Word . . ." and through the word the thought was made manifest, so that the writer should be concerned with his prose and allow his lessons to emerge from the rightness of his or her words and the vision they projected.

There are many ways in which the writers here discussed — Clark Blaise, Hugh Hood, John Metcalf, Alice Munro, and Sheila Watson — show the characteristic signs of modernist influence: in their close concern for the texture of prose; in their quasi-Imagist awareness of the revealing detail; in their interest — a varying one indeed — in verbal experimentation and their desire to "make it new" in the sense of presenting fresh and individual visions; and perhaps, most of all, in what André Gide would have called their *disponibilité*, their freedom of commitment to extraliterary bonds and preconceptions, their clear-eyed openness to experience. Political insights may *emerge* from their works, as they do, for example, from Hood's *You Cant Get There From Here* and from Metcalf's *General Ludd*, with all the Stendhalian emphasis of "a pistol-shot in the middle of a concert, something loud and vulgar, and yet a thing to which it is not possible to refuse one's attention."[3] But one does not consider Hood or Metcalf as primarily political novelists since they have not started off with the intent of teaching political lessons. The lessons have emerged after the event, as it were: from the novelists' observation of the effect of politics on human behaviour and human destiny.

In the same way, it is impossible to associate any of these writers with nationalist intentions, as one can associate an earlier novelist like Hugh MacLennan, who deliberately set out to exemplify in books like *Two Solitudes* and *The Return of the Sphinx* the problems of Canadian identity and unity; nor can one view any of them from a regionalist standpoint, as one can so many other Canadian writers of their generation. Sheila Watson made a point I think could be made for all when she said that writing *The Double Hook* began "in answer to a challenge that you could not write about particular places in Canada: that what you'd end up with was a regional novel of some kind."[4] It was a very modernist viewpoint: that by faithfully rendering the particular, one touches the universal without the need for any mediating factor like the region or the nation. That is, of course, a debatable attitude, based on a highly personal and almost solipsist attitude towards vision, and I do not share it unreservedly, but I think it more or less works for the five writers we are considering.

Some of them, indeed, are very localized in the places they write about: Sheila Watson rendering in *The Double Hook* her long-ago experience of Dog Creek, British Columbia; Alice Munro writing all her best work about the seedy town edges of southern Ontario, where she grew up; and Hugh Hood concentrating much of his fiction in his longtime home of Montreal. Others are broader in their choice of terrain, Clark Blaise usually alternating between Florida and Canada but sometimes venturing as far as India, and John Metcalf continually reverting to his English past while also writing in the Canadian present. What unites them is the sharp and concrete particularity with which experience is rendered wherever it takes place, and the particularity of experience is one of the essential assumptions of modernism.

Equally essential to modernism, whether in literature or in the visual arts, is an assumption of the universal validity, and therefore the universal availability, of form. This made the masters of the movement choose their own masters with the splendid eclecticism that so enriches *The Waste Land* and the *Four Quartets*, the *Cantos* and *Ulysses*, and *The Apes of God*.

The same might be said of the five writers represented in this volume. To begin, one of their most striking common characteristics is their apparent lack of models among Canadian writers. Undoubtedly they have been stimulated by the energies that since the 1950s have created in Canada an ambiance favourable to literature of a kind unknown before. Relatively easy publication in books and periodicals, an emergent body of intelligent critics, and a growing audience provide the kind of setting in which writers can operate with increasing confidence. But such confidence also leads writers away from the special preoccupations and problems of a nascent literature.

Nobody is concerned any longer, like poets earlier in the century, with expressing Canadian experience in its own authentic language or, as Grove was in the Prairies or Buckler in the Maritimes, with bringing an undescribed landscape, an uncelebrated pioneer way of living, into literature. These basic functional problems and the worst economic problems of publishing having been solved to the satisfaction of everyone except Robin Mathews, Canadian writing has become increasingly free to variegate, to find its own ways in content and style, and now the kind of writers who were once seen as models, like Hugh MacLennan and Morley Callaghan and W.O. Mitchell, have in fact turned into hindering and increasingly ignored stereotypes.

Keith Garebian, for example, remarks that Hugh Hood

> does not invite comparison with Canadian literary predeces-
> sors or contemporaries, but this is not because of any colonial
> romanticism or vain self-aggrandizement. It is simply because
> he does not believe that there has been any Canadian writer
> good enough to have served as an influence.[5]

And, disproportionate though Hugh Hood's opinion of himself may often seem to be, the fact is that, with the possible exception of a slight touch of Callaghan, one can detect no identifiable influence of any other Canadian writer in his work. There are times when he and Mordecai Richler may seem to echo each other, but that is almost certainly because of the experience of Montreal which these two nearly exact contemporaries, born in 1928 and 1931 respectively, have shared from different viewpoints, one Anglo-French Catholic and the other half-assimilated Jewish.

In fact, in the case of every writer discussed in this volume, the important formative influences and the important role models have been those of foreign writers. The study of Wyndham Lewis, that accidental Canadian and great international modernist, has been

Sheila Watson's most enduring preoccupation. Hugh Hood looks to Marcel Proust as the greatest novelist of modern times and describes *A la recherche du temps perdu* as "the modern epic of the individual consciousness which aims at the discovery of the fundamental laws governing the human mind."[6] Alice Munro, though her characters speak in the vernacular of southern Ontario, has found her strongest affinities in American writers like James Agee and particularly Eudora Welty. Barry Cameron remarks of Clark Blaise that

> . . . the literary and philosophical tradition to which Blaise feels the greatest affinity is neither Canadian nor American but what he has called "the discursive tradition," "literature compounded of cold observation *and* subjective passion," in sensibility if not completely in fact a French tradition: Pascal, Flaubert, Proust, Céline, Mann, and Kerouac, among others.[7]

John Metcalf, like most of the other four writers, has always been annoyed at attempts to find Canadian models for his work, and, as Douglas Rollins points out, he has declared in an interview with Barry Cameron that

> writing is an international business. There is no such thing as a national literature. . . . The influences are from whoever is good and whoever is being innovative anywhere.[8]

Elsewhere Metcalf has argued that "we need foreign models . . . ,"[9] and one of the most interesting and important passages in Rollins' essay is that in which he takes the argument back to the matter of modernist affinities with which I began this Introduction and suggests how "Metcalf's early admiration of the Imagist poets and their principles established the base from which all his work has developed." What he goes on to say about the manner in which Metcalf shows the influence of the Imagists applies also in broad terms to the other writers discussed in this chapter:

> Metcalf's rejection of abstraction (in an interview he echoed the cry "No ideas but in things"), the precision and economy of his prose, and his sensitivity to the sound and rhythmic flow

as well as the meaning of words illustrate the degree to which his practice squares with Imagist theory.[10]

Clear and particular vision, precise and economic prose, and a care for its sound and texture, plus a sharp individuality of vision, are the characteristics which all our five writers share. Reading them one has a sense that they are constantly exploring not only the human mind and the universal order it reflects, but also the language itself, and this generates a kind of participatory excitement.

Modernism, of course, is no longer the sharp spearhead of the literary avant-garde; that role has been taken over in notably various ways by the post-modernists, who have been emerging — and often vanishing — with considerable rapidity over recent years, and who often seem devoted to experiment as an activity so autonomous that its results often pass far beyond the ever-refined precision demanded by modernism into realms of esoteric obscurity the modernists would have found repellent. In such experiment for experiment's sake, none of the present writers has indulged. Even John Metcalf does not carry the principle of "No ideas but in things" to the extent of French *choseistes* like Alain Robbe-Grillet, for whom the things became so important that persons were reduced to their reflections. And the kind of inventive mingling of genres and even arts practised by Canadian writers like Michael Ondaatje, bpNichol, and bill bissett, who experiment in the areas between prose and verse and between the visual and the verbal, has not attracted any of the writers now being discussed. They are fiction writers, and if they derive techniques from other genres, as Metcalf, and I suspect also Watson, did from Imagist poetry, then these are turned to fictional ends. They experiment with a purpose, which is to make their prose more precise and revelatory, not for the sake of experiment itself, and this often means that their structures, as distinct from their textures, tend to be traditional where, as in the case of Alice Munro, for example, the traditional framework continues to be serviceable. Classic modernism, as T.S. Eliot and its other exponents made clear, never involved a mindlessly complete rejection of tradition.

Modernism, of course, was never a closely linked school of writers dominated by a clearly defined theoretical approach like Surrealism or Black Mountain poetry-writing, even though it did include in its broad scope short-lived groups with special aims like the Imagists and the Vorticists. The movement was a matter of shared attitudes rather than shared techniques, which was why it embraced figures so various as T.S. Eliot and James Joyce, as Herbert Read and Wyndham Lewis, as H.D. and Richard Aldington and Ezra Pound. These writers certainly knew each other, and each in his or her own way sought to "make it new," but they worked in increasing isolation. And the late modernist approach, shared in Canada by writers as various as Louis Dudek, the McGill poets, and the prose writers in this book, is manifest in links between writers which are those of affinity rather than of any kind of formal alliance.

It is true that for a while John Metcalf, Clark Blaise, and Hugh Hood, with other writers, were associated in The Montreal Story-tellers Fiction Performance Group, but this was less a literary coterie in the classic sense than a kind of missionary effort aimed at organizing prose readings to spread awareness of Canadian writings and writers through the educational system. It is perhaps equally significant that *White Pelican*, the Edmonton literary magazine, whose most active editor was Sheila Watson, appears to have included no contributions from Hugh Hood, John Metcalf, Alice Munro, or Clark Blaise. These writers in no way put themselves together; yet juxtaposed, by editorial fiat, they fit in with each other amazingly well.

If they are not a school, they do not form a generation either in the temporal sense, for Sheila Watson, born in 1909, is thirty-one years older than Clark Blaise (born in 1940) and twenty-nine years older than John Metcalf (born in 1938). But affinities, in Canadian writing at least, do not always go by age groups. It is too new a tradition for seniority patterns to have imposed themselves. Thus poets like Earle Birney, Dorothy Livesay, and P.K. Page, returning with a second wind at what to ordinary people would be retirement age, have astonished us by writing verse so new and contemporary that it stands admirably beside the poetry much younger people were writing at the same time. In a similar way, Sheila Watson's austerely scanty production of one small novel and five short stories, most of them written almost a quarter of a century ago, still appear with extraordinary freshness and individuality among later works by much younger writers.

Sheila Watson is the writer in this group who has the most direct links with the classic modernist movement because of her long and sustained interest in Wyndham Lewis and the fact that she first began to study him under his student and associate, Marshall McLuhan. Expressed in this way, it sounds as if one were claiming an apostolic succession, but Watson's own works are the evidence of the permeative influence of the earliest modernists, and of the Imagist poets — H.D. perhaps even more than Pound — as well as of Lewis.

Stephen Scobie says that "the major fact about Sheila Watson's biography is that she does not have one; or, rather, that she would regard it as irrelevant."[11] Doubtless, indeed, biography is irrelevant to the extent that Watson is in no sense an autobiographical writer, and therefore there is no point in seeking in her life the parallels to what her imagination has produced in the way of fiction. Yet two biographical facts do remain of crucial importance. One is that almost obsessive interest in Lewis, the author-artist whose writings were always permeated with the visuality and the imagery that came from his other life as a painter. The other is the vital two years she spent teaching during the 1930s in the little lost village of Dog Creek in the Cariboo ranching country.

At Dog Creek she was among people who lived a stark and deprived life in close contact with often violent natural forces; it was a setting of sharp, hard visual images as well as of powerful and often negative human emotions, and it stayed in her mind until it finally emerged as the subject for an only novel that was also a masterpiece and virtually — in Canadian terms — an immediate classic. In recollection, as Scobie quotes, she said of the Dog Creek experience and its relation to *The Double Hook*,

I'd been away for a long time before I realised that if I had something to say, it was going to be said in these images. And there was something I wanted to say: about how people are driven, how if they have no art, how if they have no tradition, how if they have no ritual, they are driven in one of two ways, either towards violence or towards insensibility — if they have no mediating rituals which manifest themselves in what I suppose we call art forms.[12]

Explanations of any work of art in terms of a theoretical approach tend to take one away from a real sense of the work itself, its atmosphere and its vision, from the archetypal figures like Mrs. Potter, the old fisherwoman, and James, her son and murderer, and Greta, her daughter, who burns the house and herself rather than letting either be possessed by strangers, and holy Felix, and blinded voyeur Kip, whose inner selves stumble in ignorance, shadowed by the evil will of Coyote. They move in and out of a bright mythological light and yet, at the same time, in outward appearance, are the kind of cattle-raising people one might encounter any day riding on the back roads of the Cariboo country. The clue that unites the theory and the achievement lies in the phrase "these images."

For though there have inevitably been eager scholars seeking the symbolic patterns in *The Double Hook*, Sheila Watson was not really one of those who walked through Baudelaire's *forêt de symboles*. The symbolic pattern in the novel is simple: the fish of Christian, and Coyote of Indian, mythology. The double hook itself, I would say, is emblematic rather than symbolic, a sharply visual presentation of the rival forces in the hook and their interdependence: "That when you fish for the glory you catch the darkness too. That if you hook twice the glory you hook twice the fear."[13] But, for the most part, the book is carried in the dense pattern of its images, which allow an extreme minimalization of the discursive element in the prose, for they cohere as naturally as images in a haiku:

James turned on his heel. But when he turned, he saw nothing but the water-hole and the creek and the tangle of branches which grew along it.

Ara went down the path, stepping over the dried hoofmarks down to the creek's edge. She, too, saw nothing now except a dark ripple and the padded imprint of a coyote's foot at the far edge of the moving water.

She looked up the creek. She saw the twisted feet of the cottonwoods shoved naked into the stone bottom where the water moved, and the matted branches of the stunted willow. She saw the shallow water plocking over the roots of the cottonwood, transfiguring bark and stone.

She bent towards the water. Her fingers divided it. A stone breathed in her hand. Then life drained to its centre.[14]

The cumulation of images, and the very clarity with which they are seen, builds up to a climactic part of the novel. They are used not merely for descriptive effect; each has its correlation to the emotions that are moving between people and leading to fatal action. Here and there Watson breaks with strict Imagist theory by introducing a simile: *like* is a word used quite often. But even then, the simile is so sharply visualized that it reinforces the pattern of images.

Nothing like *The Double Hook* had been written in Canada before. Its effect on younger writers has been permeative and persistent, though critics were first reluctant to recognize it. In 1977, when I said that *The Double Hook* was "one of the most important books for itself and in terms of influence" published in the 1950s,[15] I was reproved by no less a figure than Sheila Watson's fellow neo-modernist, Louis Dudek. But many of the younger critics clearly agree with me. Frank Davey recently described *The Double Hook* as "the first truly modern Canadian novel,"[16] and Stephen Scobie puts the point in an equally impressive way when he says, "Speaking for myself, both as a writer and as a critic, it is the Sheila Watson generation that I belong to."

Sheila Watson's own claims for the work, in keeping with her austere view of selfhood, have been much more modest. As we have seen, she says she wrote *The Double Hook* "in answer to a challenge that you could not write about particular places in Canada: that what you'd end up with was a regional novel of some kind."[17] That, of course, is another way of stating the important truth modernism gave to literature: that in close attention to the particular you arrive at the universal, with no need for mediation — the "World in a grain of sand" of that great pre-modernist William Blake.

It would be hard to find a greater contrast than that which one perceives between Sheila Watson and Hugh Hood: she modest in claims and works, he voluminous and somewhat vain. Except for one story that got left out, Watson's life's work — apart from *The Double Hook* — fits into a single 190-page special issue of *Open Letter*. At the last count I made, Hood had published six volumes of short stories, two volumes of essays, a book on ice hockey, and one on Seymour Segal's painting, four individual novels, and the first five volumes of his "prose epic," The New Age/Le nouveau siècle, whose various parts, he has promised us, will keep on appearing until the twelfth volume in the millennial year 2000. I am the last man to throw stones through the walls of the glass house where I live by objecting to a writer being prolific, yet I know from experience the perils that gift may involve; one of them is a diffusion of intent.

Such a diffusion emerges in Hood's various attempts, as quoted by Keith Garebian, to define his roles as a writer. He sees himself as "an epic novelist, a maker of catalogues and encyclopedias and compendia of syntax-forms, and vocabularies of names and a story teller and etc.,"[18] and again as "*both* a realist and a transcendentalist allegorist,"[19] and again as "a moral realist, not a naturalist nor a surrealist . . . or *avant-garde* writer."[20] The most obviously appropriate of these copious self-descriptions is that of the "maker of catalogues and encyclopedias" for the immediately striking feature of Hood's stories and novels — and even of the putative prose epic, The New Age — is the remarkable sense of the detail of everyday life presented with what Frank Davey once called "invisible craftsmanship." Davey went on to say that Hood's work "gives the illusion of being journalistic reportage — chatty, matter of fact, and unplanned; the casual voice of a somewhat unsophisticated but sensible narrator can be heard throughout. . . . the reader is led to trust every detail that Hood offers."[21]

And the detail comes in abundance, for Hood, even if he makes no claims to being an "*avant-garde* writer," is a modernist at least in his devotion to the particular as a means of approaching the universal. Garebian takes Robert Fulford to task for his definition of Hood as "a superior journalist" being "slowly strangled by an inferior novelist."[22] Yet part of Fulford's statement is obviously true. Hood does excel in those very activities he shares with journalists and special historians: the precise detailing of the actual process of living. No novelist — Canadian or other — whom I know of enters so subtly into the occupational lives of his characters and describes them with such precise and convincing detail; but Hood is by no means so convincing when he enters the emotional lives of the same people, which he tends to see *sub specie aeternitatis* rather than in diurnal terms, and therefore not quite humanly. Garebian is quite right to say that "as a didactic writer, Hood has few equals anywhere,"[23] but didacticism is no unequivocal virtue for a writer, and in Hood's work it introduces a discursive Victorian element that clashes with the modernist urge to deal with people and their relationships, which are the stuff of novels, in terms of the concrete and particular imagery he applies to the material framework of their lives.

Looking through the volumes of his dodecalogy, The New Age, that have so far appeared, it seems as though Hood's problems are partly those of the culture to which he belongs. For this "prose epic," which we were led to believe might be the North American equivalent of Proust's masterpiece, in fact resembles it in only two ways: it is long; and its narrator and protagonist is obviously one of the author's personae, so that it is virtually, if not literally, autobiographical. But the texture of The New Age, its cultural substantiality, its explorations into the rhythms of human minds and feelings, and even the quality of its presentation of a living society, fall so far short of the great European fictional epics, like Ulysses and A la recherche du temps perdu, that one is led to assume such works can only successfully be written in the context of ancient and elaborate cultural traditions, traditions moreover at the point of decay.

It is significant in this connection that the first and still the best work of modernist fiction written in Canada — The Double Hook — should have been short and concise (a poetic novella rather than a novel in the true sense), that Hood's own best works so far should be the stories, where his talent for precise, quasi-reportorial detail can best be deployed, and that the three remaining writers discussed in this volume should all be primarily short-story writers whose novels show in their episodic structures a continuing adherence to the shorter form.

Alice Munro is one of those writers who at first sight appear to be working in a style of clear and lucid realism — the style that critics find it hardest to deal with since everything seems so precisely and naturally there. But very soon one becomes aware of the forms moving beneath that translucent surface, so that, as Hallvard Dahlie says of the stories in Dance of the Happy Shades, one finds oneself facing "a recognizably realistic world whose components never leave one entirely comfortable, a situation rendered both ambivalent and complex by Munro's sensitive use of irony, paradox, and understatement."[24] And as one goes further on into Munro's writing career, one finds that, as with some abstract painters, what is absent becomes as important as what is there. What Dahlie terms "the inability to communicate, the reduction to silences, [and] the futility of words" become unavoidable elements in the process of actual communication between writer and reader as well as factors of noncommunication between characters: so much in these splendid stories goes by implication.

This is why Alice Munro, since she became established as a writer, has always made a dual appeal. On the one hand, she is in Canadian terms a best-seller, even achieving publication by large paperback houses in the United States, and that is because of the immediate, on-the-surface appeal of her books, in which readers — and women especially — find that she is presenting what in realistic terms seem to be situations with which they can identify, and is reflecting their own perplexities when they come to realize, as Dahlie puts it, "that morality itself is an elusive aspect of reality, and that human relationships create by their very interaction a perpetually shifting dimension of this morality." On the other hand, Munro has always been admired by her fellow writers for the extraordinary lucidity of her prose, for her precise handling of sensual data, and for her skilful use of the short-story form in its most effective way — again in Dahlie's words — "to attach added intensity to the dilemmas her protagonists face, or, perhaps more accurately, to leave them with those tensions suspended that a novel more typically would resolve."

If Alice Munro combines rather enviably the two roles of a moderately popular story writer and a writer's writer, both Clark Blaise and John Metcalf, with their deliberate and at times rather vocal preoccupation with the problems of the literary artist, are still very much writers' writers, as the great modernists of course also were until history lifted them on its tide by turning them into classics and therefore indispensable reading.

Clark Blaise's work largely derives its interest from the fact that it belongs in a middle land of fiction between the short story and the novel. Even in what look like collections of short stories, such as *A North American Education* and *Tribal Justice*, there will be groups of items with a common central character, and this character will provide the continuity in what would otherwise be a discontinuous world, a "culturally disparate" world as Barry Cameron describes it,[25] whose divisions are symbolized by the divided origins and loyalties of the central figure, and by the geographical dispersion of the action; there are always journeys to be made, roads to be followed to indefinite destinations.

The sense of alienation, of being a stranger in a strange world, that has been so strong in the French writers Blaise admires — from Pascal (another Blaise!) down to Alain-Fournier and Camus — is carried in his writing perhaps farther than in the work of any other Canadian writer. Everywhere he is dealing with outsiders — Floridans in Montreal, Montrealers in the South, North Americans in India — but the outsider status is as much spiritual as geographical. And, through the compelling confidentiality with which Blaise writes, that status is made universal as well. Blaise is virtually telling the reader, as Barry Cameron remarks, ". . . you too are a voyeur; you too are forever an alien." Yet there is more to these strange books than mere alienation, for one of the essential characteristics of the voyeur, after all, is that he *sees*. And if Blaise writes largely, as he has said, of a world in which so much is a matter "of the sinister and of duplicities and dualities,"[26] he is still a revealer of mysteries; and, as Dennis Duffy has said, ". . . the essential theme of exploration and delicate adjustment, concluded often with a vision of loneliness, abides throughout his work."[27]

John Metcalf is an interesting mixture of the high artist and the satirist, which means that he combines a strong element of the didactic with his formal preoccupations. We have already seen how resistant he is to any nationalist approach to literature, how he sees writing as international and his own roots going down wherever good writing is being done. He has also declared, in refreshing exception to the pseudopopulist trends of the time, "I want to write elitist art. It's the austere that appeals to me more than anything else in art" (Cameron, p. 411).

Metcalf's derivations from Imagism, already noted, have led him into a sharp prose in which particulars are carefully recorded and almost mosaically constructed into the frameworks of episodes whose placing together becomes an important structural element in his work. The short story, a clear and quickly apprehensible frame of incident, is both the form he likes most and the one in which his particular gifts as an artificer of fiction are perhaps best used.

He has always resented the conventions of the ordinary traditional novel. Douglas Rollins appositely quotes Barry Cameron's interview with Metcalf, in which he intimated that the episodic structure of his first novel, *Going Down Slow*, resulted from his impatience at "having to put connecting bits in and continuing the story. It was the set pieces of the book . . . that [he] really enjoyed because they were the closest to the short story form" (Cameron, p. 403). Metcalf has made no bones about the deliberate character of his writing, no pretence of writing "naturally." It is all avowedly artifice and manipulation, both of the prose and of the readers' reactions. And so he could admit frankly to Cameron that he started on *Going Down Slow* largely because he had been told that writing a novel would further his career.

But, despite the episodic character of *Going Down Slow*, this novel and its successor, *General Ludd*, do add up to a great deal more than episodic sequences, since it is in these books that Metcalf's comic and satiric gifts have emerged. He has said — like Orwell — that ". . . all writing is political, all great writing subversive,"[28] which means that, despite his concern for the artifice of writing, he adopts no narrowly aestheticist stand. His books are intended, if not to teach, certainly at times to preach, and he is quite ready to use his sharp-edged prose to expose the flaws of a society he largely despises. *Going Down Slow*, essentially a fictional attack on the Canadian educational system, reminds one in more than its title of the "angry young men" who were prominent in England during Metcalf's boyhood there, but it is in *General Ludd* that he really comes into his own, using his talent for creating convincing episodes to construct a true picaresque, the ideal form for a comic fiction. *General Ludd* is a book of outlandish imagery and scornful prose, in many ways reminiscent of Céline's masterpieces, *Voyage au bout de la nuit* and *Mort à crédit*, and like those books it offers, as John Moss has said, "a vision that is at once hilarious and chilling" in its exposure of a society dying for the lack of art. Moss considers it "probably the finest comic novel ever published in Canada,"[29] and such perhaps it is, if one excepts Wyndham Lewis' *Self Condemned*, which, though about Canada, was first published elsewhere.

I have no reason for suggesting that *General Ludd* may have been influenced by *Self Condemned*, but there are strong parallels between the views the two novels present of the philistine ugliness of Canadian urban existence and the hollow pretentiousness of its academic life. And it seems appropriate to end by pointing out the affinities of a contemporary Canadian novelist with the classic modernist who indirectly, through Sheila Watson, contributed to the modern trend in Canadian fiction.

NOTES

[1] *Canadian Writers and Their Works*, ed. Robert Lecker, Jack David, and Ellen Quigley, Fiction ser., VII (Toronto, ECW, 1985), pp. 217–18; hereafter cited as *CWTW*.

[2] *CWTW*, Fiction ser., VII, pp. 262–63.

[3] This description by Stendhal of "politics in a work of literature" is quoted in Irving Howe, *Politics and the Novel* (New York: Meridian, 1957), p. 15.

[4] Sheila Watson, "What I'm Going to Do," *Open Letter*, 3rd ser., No. 1 (Winter 1974–75) [*Sheila Watson: A Collection*], 182.

[5] *CWTW*, Fiction ser., VII, pp. 98–99.

[6] Pierre Cloutier, "An Interview with Hugh Hood," *Journal of Canadian Fiction*, 2, No. 1 (Winter 1973), 52.

[7] *CWTW*, Fiction ser., VII, p. 27.

[8] Barry Cameron, "The Practice of the Craft: A Conversation with John Metcalf," *Queen's Quarterly*, 82 (Autumn 1975), 412–13. All further references to this work (Cameron) appear in the text.

[9] John Metcalf and Clark Blaise, Introd., *Here and Now*, ed. John Metcalf and Clark Blaise (Ottawa: Oberon, 1977), p. 6.

[10] Douglas Rollins, "John Mecalf (1938–)," in *CWTW*, Fiction ser., VII, p. 167.

[11] *CWTW*, Fiction ser., VII, p. 259.

[12] Watson, "What I'm Going to Do," p. 183.

[13] Sheila Watson, *The Double Hook* (Toronto: McClelland and Stewart, 1959), pp. 4–6.

[14] Watson, *The Double Hook*, p. 29.

[15] George Woodcock, "Possessing the Land: Notes on Canadian Fiction," in *The Canadian Imagination: Dimensions of a Literary Culture*, ed. David Staines (Cambridge: Harvard Univ. Press, 1977), pp. 93–94.

[16] Frank Davey, "Watson, Sheila," in *The Oxford Companion to Canadian Literature*, ed. William Toye (Toronto: Oxford Univ. Press, 1983), p. 822.

[17] Watson, "What I'm Going to Do," p. 182.

[18] "Hugh Hood and John Mills in Epistolary Conversation," *The Fiddlehead*, No. 116 (Winter 1978), p. 136.

[19] "Hugh Hood and John Mills in Epistolary Conversation," p. 145.

[20] Hugh Hood, "The Ontology of Super-Realism," in *The Governor's Bridge Is Closed* (Ottawa: Oberon, 1973), p. 127.

[21] Frank Davey, "Hugh Hood," in *From There to Here: A Guide to English-Canadian Literature since 1960* (Erin, Ont.: Porcépic, 1974), p. 138.

[22] Robert Fulford, "Hugh Hood's Misused Talent," rev. of *The Camera Always Lies* and *Around the Mountain*, by Hugh Hood, *Toronto Daily Star*, 11 Oct. 1967, p. 43.

[23] *CWTW*, Fiction ser., VII, p. 122.

[24] *CWTW*, Fiction ser., VII, p. 236.

[25] *CWTW*, Fiction ser., VII, p. 59.

[26] Geoff Hancock, "An Interview with Clark Blaise," *Canadian Fiction Magazine*, Nos. 34–35 (1980), p. 54.

[27] Dennis Duffy, "Blaise, Clark," in *The Oxford Companion to Canadian Literature*, ed. William Toye (Toronto: Oxford Univ. Press, 1983), p. 74.

[28] John Metcalf, "Soaping a Meditative Foot (Notes for a Young Writer)," in *The Narrative Voice: Short Stories and Reflections by Canadian Authors*, ed. John Metcalf (Toronto: McGraw-Hill Ryerson, 1972), p. 154.

[29] John Moss, *A Reader's Guide to the Canadian Novel* (Toronto: McClelland and Stewart, 1981), pp. 200, 197.

CHAPTER 8

Equations and Discordances: Mavis Gallant, Norman Levine, Audrey Thomas, Leon Rooke, Timothy Findley

WHERE LITERATURE is concerned, the urge to find significant arrangements is always present, whether it is among the writers themselves or among their critics and editors. And in writing the introductions to the volumes of *Canadian Writers and Their Works*, I began with the assumption that in offering a volume to me the editors had been led in their selection by at least a sense of affinity between the authors who were included. Thus I have always begun by trying to identify the common elements or the significant contrasts. Sometimes the pattern has emerged immediately with felicitous clarity; sometimes I have had to search hard to find it.

In the case of the present chapter, the equations are there, but almost equally strong are the discordances, which are as much of generation as of gender when one looks at this group of five, three men and two women, two of them (Mavis Gallant and Norman Levine) born in the 1920s and three of them (Audrey Thomas, Timothy Findley, and Leon Rooke) in the 1930s. One might also bring up the contrast between natives and immigrants, for Gallant and Levine are Canadian-born and Thomas and Rooke are Americans by origin. But this point is somewhat neutralized by the fact that Gallant, Findley, and Levine have lived most of their writing lives in Europe, while Thomas and Rooke have come to literary maturity in Canada, however much at times the vestiges of their American pasts may seem to cling.

I suppose the one element that does unite most of these five writers is a matter of formal preference; though they have written novels, novellas, and stories, they seem with one exception to be most successful in the briefer structures. But in each case, this success may be rather deceptive, for the difficulties evident in their longer works can be rewarding even in their often imperfect solutions, since these works represent serious attempts to grapple with the role of fiction in our age when writers still hover between modernism and post-modernism, between realism and metafiction, and are enriched rather than diminished by the range of possibilities. Timothy Findley is the exception, best in large structures linked to history or myth.

One can divide the writers here presented in two different ways apart from generation and gender. First there are those — Levine and Thomas — who are engaged in that haunted borderland between autobiography and fiction which has attracted many writers at least since Aphra Behn wrote *Oroonoko; or, The Royal Slave* (1688) by transmuting and embellishing the experiences of her childhood in Guiana. It is a borderland that some of us, like the present writer, have known from the autobiographical side: how much, in a successful memoir, actual experience must be rearranged and essentially fictionalized to make it authentic. Writers like Levine and Thomas pick up on the other side of the interface and constantly arrange and fictionalize material taken from their own experience.

Yet there is an obvious difference between a writer like Norman Levine, who adopts something very like the original documentary approach of Daniel Defoe, presenting what purports to be a straightforward narrative of ordinary existence, and one like Audrey Thomas, who is ready to use any metafictional or surrealist technique she can lay her mind on to project what in the end seems to her the most intriguing literary problem of all — the extent to which, in trying to remain faithful to art as well as experience, the writer is forced to adopt devices that inevitably remove her or him from the realm of actuality and even from that of veracity. Thomas once said — and who among us can refute her? — "Writers are terrible liars. There are nicer names for it, of course, but liars will do. They take a small incident and blow it up, like a balloon. . . ."[1] They also find, if they are writers like Thomas, with notable literary erudition and a recognition of the way in which the act of writing becomes a closed, self-reflexive process, that even if they have not adopted the extreme aestheticist doctrine of art for art's sake, they are involved in a process where the true presentation of feeling becomes entangled with the postmodernist problems of literary communication; with endlessly equivocal relations among character, writer, and reader, that *"hypocrite lecteur"* who, as Baudelaire saw so long ago, is the unpredictable joker in any literary game.

If the writing of Levine and Thomas derives so much from personal experience, presented plain by Levine and coloured by Thomas, both Gallant and Rooke rely far more on worlds of the imagination outside direct personal experience. But here also there is a clear division which mirrors that between Levine and Thomas. Gallant may not — except in the Linnet Muir stories — examine her own personal life, but she does rely greatly on her perceptions of a world she regards with constant curiosity, creating characters and situations out of fugitive and fragmentary encounters and chance-heard conversations, so that it is hard to tell in her stories where observation ends and invention begins. What she shares with Leon Rooke is the fact that her own life is not the palpable centre of her fictional world; she faces, and in her own way deals with, the problem of otherness by making it the basis of her fictional approach, which rests essentially on the creation of alienated characters in a great variety of predicaments.

But Gallant differs from Rooke, as Levine does from Thomas, in the sense that in broad terms — the terms of Flaubert in one case and Graham Greene in the other — they are both realists. They set out to create and to portray with appropriate artifice the lives of credible people who may or may not resemble their authors. Plausibility and verisimilitude are old-fashioned goals they retain as the great premodernist literary masters did before them. Proust would recognize a kindred spirit in his admirer Gallant, and Gissing, I suspect, would acknowledge a fellow in Levine.

I do not suggest that Gallant and Levine ignore the problems of communicating through writing or the ambiguities of the relations between the writer and his literary predecessors or between the writer and his readers; occasionally, in fact, as in her novella "The Pegnitz Junction," Gallant does seem, in her playful parody of contemporary German writers and in her manipulation of telepathic awareness, to be encroaching on metafictional and extrarational areas of post-modernism where Thomas and Rooke are more evidently comfortable. But she and Levine clearly regard these problems mainly as challenges to their skills and assume that by writing clearly and well, they can communicate their insights and stir their readers' imaginations. To writers like Thomas and Rooke, on the other hand, the problems of communication, and the sense that writing is an autonomous activity, fed by life yet in some way self-perpetuating and self-modifying, can never be avoided, though this does not mean that their work is without moral, as well as aesthetic, content.

Norman Levine is the least immediately spectacular of these writers. He offers a plain and unembellished prose; his people tend to sadden, rather than inspire, one with their resigned ineffectuality. If they seem at times affirmative or assertive, we feel it to be out of character; at best one can say of them, as Lawrence Mathews does, that they show "awkward incompleteness paradoxically linked with dignity."[2] Levine's admiration for Graham Greene, which led him to entitle his one travel book *Canada Made Me* in a none too oblique tribute, emerges in a shared preoccupation with "the failures, . . . the seedy."[3] In comparison with the highly imaginative and sometimes exotic fiction of the four other writers we are discussing, his stories seem flat in tone and often banal in conception. His prose never lacks in clarity, and, as Mathews remarks, he always seems to be "speaking in his own voice," with no metafictional trickery, and he would probably reject with some indignation Thomas' view of the writer as liar. He early came to the conclusion that, again to quote Mathews, ". . . poetry can be discovered in precise observation of the ordinary . . . ,"[4] and in fiction the ordinary remained his province. His rejection of avant-gardism of any kind probably marks him off from most of his contemporaries. His rather staid and old-fashioned realism is shown in his admiration for Graham Greene because Greene showed so clearly the "visible world" around one, and in his preference for the Joyce of "The Dead" over the Joyce of *Ulysses*.

Levine's writing has indeed been so evasively modest that even his admirers, at least in Canada, find it hard to pick the right words to praise him. Robert Weaver, with the best will in the world, ended up writing an essentially neutral account of him in *The Oxford*

Companion to Canadian Literature. Frank Davey rather pointedly left him out of his "guide to English-Canadian literature since 1960," *From There to Here,* and W.J. Keith could find only faint praise for him in his recent *Canadian Literature in English.*

But there is no doubt that something in Levine's unassuming writing at times, as I once remarked, "stirs one's empathies and quietly saddens one."[5] Margaret Keith in her piece on him in *Contemporary Novelists* remarks perceptively that his language is "so empty of implication that it becomes mysterious," and she adds:

In his low-keyed world even tiny incidents stand out like figures against a landscape of snow. They may mean nothing or anything, but to him they have an importance which the reader feels, but never entirely understands.[6]

Perhaps it is this inadvertent mystery that explains the curious fact of Levine's considerable reputation in both West and East Germany in comparison with the low-keyed approval he has received in both Canada and England. Of course, the reputations that English-speaking writers have acquired in continental Europe often bear little relation to the intrinsic merits of their writing. Byron and Wilde were both esteemed more than their literary betters because the exile into which their lifestyles forced them seemed a reproach to Perfidious Albion. Mazo de la Roche in her day was far better known in France than any Québécois writer because her facile romancing struck a responsive popular cord. Edgar Allan Poe gained a vast French reputation through the advocacy of Baudelaire, and there seems little doubt that Levine owes his success in Germany largely to the good fortune that his work attracted the attention of Heinrich Böll, who actually became his translator. And what may have attracted Böll was a prose so clear and neutral, and so lacking in idiomatic individuality, that it could be easily rendered into German.

Mathews speaks well for Levine but perhaps weakens his advocacy by sometimes claiming too much. He objects to Terry Goldie's remark that ". . . the major writer must have major things to say. Levine does not."[7] Mathews goes on to suggest that Levine's later writings do bring in what one might regard as major themes, such as freedom. But to be a major writer, one does not have only to enunciate in some unobtrusive way one or more of the grand human themes. One has to enunciate them in a major way, and there is nothing in the forms or the concepts or the language of Levine's writing that has enough originality or grandeur to seem in any true way "major." Change a word, and what Archibald Lampman once said of himself could best define Levine: "I am a minor poet of a superior order, and that is all."[8] And that, for most writers, in the end is enough.

The richness and complexity that Mavis Gallant has given to the short story can only be seen in terms of contrast to the grey understatement of Levine's fiction. Which is not to accuse Gallant of overstatement, but to draw attention to the variety and depth of perception and the range of expression shown in the hundred-odd stories and the handful of novels and novellas she has published since she set out in 1950 for her long and chosen exile in Europe.

Gallant's realism is much more than a matter of presenting plausible settings or even of creating credible speech patterns for an astonishing variety of characters, though she does both with great virtuosity. It is essentially a psychological realism, and there is nothing accidental about the fact that Marcel Proust is Gallant's favourite author. Psychological realism, as I see it, differs from the naturalist realism of a writer like Levine in that it is responsive to what Proust used to call the "intermittencies of the heart" and is therefore much more fluid in its handling of time and much more experimental in its rendering of memory. So, while Gallant may seem straightforward in her prose, she is in fact very subtle in the variations she achieves in the patterns of spoken and unspoken speech, and in the devices she employs to create the temporal patterns of her fictions, particularly in her longer stories, and in her novels, like *A Fairly Good Time*, in which a variety of devices — journals, letters, interior monologues, and recollective flashbacks — are used very skilfully to illuminate the central story of the failure of a marriage between a Canadian girl and a member of a stuffily conservative French family. Judith Skelton Grant writes interestingly on the "circling structures," the "loops," by which, in so many of the stories, time comes back on itself so that a formal, as well as a psychological, ordering of the story is created.[9]

What emerges from such structures is an order that avoids

continuity, and this accords with Gallant's belief — perhaps not derived from, but certainly resembling, Proust's "intermittencies" — that life is discontinuous and not a tightly knit structure of cause and effect; such a belief has made her happier, and better, with the short story than with the longer fictional forms.

The sense of life as discontinuous already introduces a kind of alienation, from one's past, from one's other selves, and undoubtedly it is connected closely with the fact that, as Grant remarks, "exile, expatriation, and rootlessness" become "recurrent in [Gallant's] fiction."[10] We have already seen alienation, in the form of a difficulty in entering a foreign culture, as the basic theme of her larger and more successful novel. And the sense of being a stranger, often unable to make adjustments to the home that destiny has chosen for one, is recurrent in her stories.

Of course, this feeling of alienation and impermanence echoes far back into Gallant's life; she says of the seventeen shifts she made in her childhood from school to school that they "did something positive for me — there's no milieu I don't feel comfortable in, that I don't immediately understand."[11] But, one begins to speculate as one reads her stories, is it really *the milieu* that she understands? Is it not rather the experience of being recurrently a stranger in new places? Admittedly she has developed an extraordinary eye for background detail, but within her meticulously observed and recorded settings, she writes better of the transient than of the inhabitant, and on the occasions when she does write well of the inhabitant, we usually find that he is somehow alien in his own country.

Thus, though her stories are frequently about Anglo-Saxons — British as well as Canadians and sometimes Americans — leading empty and often spiteful lives in France or Italy, she also shows in one of her collections, *The Pegnitz Junction*, how a whole people, the post-Nazi generation of Germany, have been alienated — not from their native land but from the past which they are trying desperately to forget. Even when she turns back to her own country and countrymen in *Home Truths*, she shows how Canadians are often "foreigners" even when they do not live abroad. The most impressive stories in this volume are the semi-autobiographical Linnett Muir pieces, and these concern the failure of a young woman, returning to Montreal, to find her emotional bearings even in the city where she was born and spent her childhood.

It may be perilous to generalize over a large group of stories that show a great variety of situation, characterization, and thematic approach, but most of Gallant's fiction does concern people who have built up some kind of protection from the world, and who in the end are made to realize how precarious their defences are against the inherent discontinuousness of existence, and how hiding from life and trying to make themselves impervious to change has only increased their vulnerability. Gallant's stories are witty and often humourous in their way of expression yet pathetic in their unfolding effect; they are detached in viewpoint, so that at times they seem positively callous, yet they are so involving that one's final emotion is always something nearer to compassion than to contempt. Gallant has sometimes been called a satirist, but the satirist writes in the hope that mankind can be reformed, whereas Gallant seems sadly to know that the people she writes of will never become wiser or better.

Many of Gallant's stories have highly complex structures, not only involving elaborate manipulations of time and memory, but also the interplay of varying points of view. Sometimes the handling of incident, the way the visible and audible world cuts away from the inner world and back again, is almost cinematic in its effect and reminds one of Gallant's early training in the National Film Board, but in other stories there is often a distinctly dramatic feeling in the arrangement of scenes and the strength of dialogue. Indeed, Gallant seems to write with a special kind of relationship to most of the other arts, for she has a sharp eye for the visible world, and her stories often take on a marvellously visual quality so that the words seem like a translucent veil over what is seen. This offers an extraordinary double effect, so that the scene is observed as clearly and concretely as the background to a Pre-Raphaelite painting, yet one is always moving through it into the characters' states of mind, which are so convincing because they are related constantly to the physical here-and-now.

Because she has lived so long away and in her early writing years published so much abroad rather than in her home country, Canadians have been slow in recognizing Gallant's excellences. In the first edition of the *Literary History of Canada: Canadian Literature in English* (1965), her name is mentioned twice, but nothing is said about her writing, and in the second edition (1976), William H. New discusses her and Levine together, presumably because they were both exile writers; I doubt if he would do the same, now we have become more aware of the power and versatility of Gallant's writing. How far we have now gone in recognizing this undeniably major writer is shown by W.J. Keith when he remarks, in *Canadian Literature in English*, on "the number of accomplished women writers who have achieved distinction since the 1950s" and then quietly adds: "Of these . . . Mavis Gallant is perhaps supreme."[12]

It is a daringly emphatic statement, but it should not be dismissed without consideration, for as a stylist Gallant's only real rival among Canadian women writers was Marian Engel, and in narrative skill and psychological insight, Gallant certainly has no superiors.

Keith notes also that in spite of Gallant's stance as "a writer in the English language" without local ties, there is "a recognizably Canadian detachment about her authorial stance," yet he credits her with being in her own special way an international writer who "has brought an uncommon polish and sophistication into the literature of her native country and has also introduced an independent Canadian perspective to the literary world of both Europe and the United States."[13] And, indeed, one has to go back to Sara Jeannette Duncan in the late nineteenth century to find a Canadian writer whose position was comparable with hers, but even Duncan could not rival Gallant's awesome fictional skill.

It was André Gide in *Les Caves du Vatican* who first developed the idea of the "*acte gratuit*," the motiveless deed, as a factor challenging the fiction bound by causality of the naturalists, like Edmond and Jules de Goncourt and Emile Zola, who had preceded him. But Gide's rebellion against the necessitarian patterns of late nineteenth-century fiction was somewhat negated by his own stylistic classicism, and though in other novels, like *Les Faux-Monnayeurs* with its elaborate mirror patterns of diaries within diaries and writers writing about writers, he anticipated the metafictional trends of recent years, there was still a disturbing quality of artifice about his attempts to project the disorderliness and discontinuity of life.

Nobody to my knowledge, and certainly not Keith Garebian in

the essay he contributed to *Canadian Writers and Their Works*, has thought of mentioning Gide in connection with Leon Rooke. But the comparison does suggest that others have been before where our post-modernists are now treading. Garebian quotes Rooke as saying: "I don't like resolving situations because most situations are not resolved. I like the open ending. I like the reader to say, 'This is the ending,' and the other reader to say, 'No, this is the ending.' "[14] André Gide would have agreed; the open-ended novel was his aim also. And when we come to the features of Rooke's work described by Garebian as "the rejection of ethical absolutes" and "the rejection of the traditional satirist's faith in the efficacy of satire as a reforming instrument," the links with the Gide of *L'Immoraliste* as well as of *Les Caves du Vatican* are clearly evident.[15]

I am not suggesting the links are direct. I have no evidence that Rooke ever read Gide, though given his academic background, it seems unlikely that he did not. But the literary background he emerged from, that of the fictional tradition of the Southern states, was essentially North American, though in its own way as permeated with decadence as the symbolist background from which Gide himself emerged. Certainly it was not Canadian, and there is no sign that past Canadian writers have influenced Rooke any more than the Canadian environment in which he has lived for almost two decades has had any deep effect on his fiction, except in liberating him from the setting of his youth and enabling him to develop at a distance the strain of writing on which he had started even before he came northward. Rooke, as Garebian points out, has deliberately dissociated himself from any definition by region: "Place (locale) in fiction," Rooke has said, is "a vastly over-rated virtue."[16]

Rooke calls himself a New Traditionalist, which means that he is quite willing to pick up traditional elements from the cultural debris in which the post-modernists like to rummage, and incorporate them into his experimental structures. Doubtless this literary scavenging has contributed to the variety and the inventive oddity which his works display, particularly as one reads the plot summaries to which Garebian devotes so much of his essay. Certainly, more than any other writer I know of in Canada, Rooke is a virtuoso of the metafictional, presenting the disorder of existence with kaleidoscopic vividness and fragmentation.

Yet, in the end, as with Gide, how much it all seems a work of brilliant contrivance! The post-moderns have never really reconciled, any more than their grandly imperfect predecessor did, their rejection of pattern in life with the acceptance of another pattern that comes inevitably when one introduces the process of fiction as subject into the fiction itself.

Such movements, it seems to me, though they are inevitably part of the general flow of literature, are side channels that eventually flow back into the mainstream and enrich it by immersion, as happened with Gongorism in seventeenth-century Spain, with the decadent movement of the *fin de siècle*, with Vorticism which spilled over from art to writing, and with surrealism. They depend too much on theory and artifice to dominate the mainstream or materially change its course, but they contribute greatly through the experimentation that originally sets them apart.

One thing a writer like Rooke demonstrates, as Gallant does in another way, is that there are standards and loyalties other than local ones. By their very presence, such artists disprove the nationalist contentions that Canadian literature must interpret Canadian life and project what purport to be Canadian values. They place our writing in the broader setting to which as work in English it also belongs.

Audrey Thomas has seized upon the best of several worlds. She is a psychological realist of — as Frank Davey once remarked — "an extreme kind," but in addition, as Davey also said, she is a "technical adventuress."[17] She has a strong natural scholarliness, which is perhaps why she never fitted into the normal academic world, and this has given her an awareness of the uses of words and literary structures that she has put to good use as she turns metafictional devices to the service of her psychological realism. In addition, she works always in the valley where autobiography and fiction come together, so that her works are never far from life but never become literal presentations. Barbara Godard says appropriately of her that, "Like many other expatriates, she has used writing to bring order to her varied existence, giving herself a context through words."[18]

In this sense, without being any less imaginative, Thomas is certainly less inventive than writers like Gallant and Rooke, who mostly portray sharply differentiated others, even if in the end, one recognizes that the others project their own potentialities. She differs from them also in defining herself as a regionalist, and, interestingly enough given her American youth and the African travels of her young womanhood, she does so in the most local way, not — as she has insisted — as a "Canadian writer," but as a "B.C. writer," celebrating in this way the fact that British Columbia has been not only the place where her writing matured, but also the setting that has inspired some of the best of her writing.

Given the fact that, in *Mrs. Blood* and elsewhere, Thomas has written often of her African experience, there is always a temptation to see her in similar terms to other Canadian writers, like Dave Godfrey and Margaret Laurence, on whose fiction periods in Africa have also had profound influence. But the resemblances are limited, for while Laurence and Godfrey were fascinated by African society and by the political developments as colonial Gold Coast changed into independent Ghana, Thomas was already concerned deeply with the way in which feminine psychology and feminine physicality reacted on each other, and with the perhaps not entirely alien subject of the process of literary creation, with its periodicities and its gestational cycles.

During the two decades since the appearance of her first book, *Ten Green Bottles* (1967), Thomas has demonstrated in her writing a great formal variety and a great range of perception. Her novels vary from the powerful study of a divided personality in *Mrs. Blood* through the almost classical *Bildungsroman* of *Songs My Mother Taught Me* to the sophisticated use of a collage technique that, in the highly experimental *Blown Figures*, perpetually invites the reader to vary the plot. In her volume of two novellas, *Munchmeyer* and *Prospero on the Island*, the post-modernist problems of the relations between writer and character, work and reader, are worked out in interlacing structures. *Munchmeyer* is a kind of mirror work in which it is hard to tell what is meant to be real action and what is the novelist hero's fantasy. The situation is complicated by the fact that *Munchmeyer* has actually been written by Miranda, the protagonist of *Prospero on the Island*, so that it is in fact a work within a work, which she discusses with Prospero, an elderly painter living on the same British Columbian island.

In Thomas' fiction, forms shade off one into the other, so that her novels take episodic shapes that resemble collections of related stories, while her stories tend to fall into linked groups. They vary over an immense range from fairy tales to studies of childhood awakening, from sharp-edged comedies of manners to troubled studies of the relationships of women and men and the relationships between women, whether they are friends or mothers and daughters. Perhaps it is the fact that she has come so honestly to a feminine viewpoint based on a recognition of sensibilities differing according to gender that has saved Thomas from falling into the arid didacticism which has marred so much feminist fiction, just as it mars any determinedly partisan writing.

Constant throughout Thomas' writing is the fact of suffering, and an acute awareness of suffering's psychological results — its power to distort perceptions and memories alike. A recurrent situation brings us — sometimes in the setting of an actual madhouse or its hospital ward equivalent — to the appalling borderland between sanity and madness, and here, in its most concentrated form, appears the terror that shadows all Thomas' fiction. Yet the essential quality of her work is not the sense of nightmare that haunts all her psychologically complex characters with their feelings of loss, their postlapsarian guilt, and their inevitably imperfect grasp of experience, but is rather the precarious balance between fear and the joy of existence which so intermittently — but more frequently and securely in her later fiction — they achieve. There are in Thomas few of the superbly "well-made" structures or of the impeccable surfaces one admires in Gallant's stories, largely because she does not seek to make her work what in a double sense she might consider "finished." She is always starting again; she herself has said, "All my novels are one novel, in a sense. . . . Each one extends, in a different style, offering more information, from a different perspective, what is basically the same story."[19] And in the process of perfecting these variations, she has taken her place among the best and least predictable of our writers.

When *Canadian Writers and Their Works* was first planned, Timothy Findley did not seem exceptional enough to rank a place among Canada's major fiction writers. The works he published during the 1980s have completely changed our view of him.

Findley actually started publishing fiction in the 1950s, with a story in the first issue of *The Tamarack Review* (1956) but during this early period he was largely involved in acting, and in several ways the theatrical career he would eventually abandon had its effect upon his later writings. His novels show him to be highly conscious of the dramatic potentialities in human relationships, and very often he seems to be moving into that area between actuality and illusion where we accept the backdrop for what it pretends to be and willingly allow the devices of *trompe-l'oeil* to go unchallenged.

Findley has published to date six novels and a couple of volumes of lapidary short stories. His novels expand into broader, looser forms, which is in keeping with his emergence as a kind of historical novelist, for history, and in particular the relationship between individual and community, is his favourite but not necessarily his most tractable material. In all his novels, whatever the vantage point, we look back into a past that for most of us is completed, finished business, but for Findley provides a stage to enact dramas in which his characters respond to the situation the world presents, accepting or reacting.

Findley's first novel, *The Last of the Crazy People*, presents the 1960s in southern California, where a child, obsessed by the futility of his family's existence in a world that wars have robbed of meaning, eventually kills the people he most loves as the merciless logics of childhood and insanity blend. In *The Butterfly Plague* he takes us to the late 1930s in Hollywood, where the fate of a family threatened by an inherited disease parallels the breakdown of civilization in Europe during the same decade.

The two great conflicts which mark off that period are the settings for Findley's major novels, *The Wars* and *Famous Last Words*, the first dominated by the senseless slaughters of what we used to call the Great War, and the second set in World War II and the bizarre and dread-ridden years leading up to it. In such novels rewriting is the key concept, for unlike past historical novelists, Findley does not seek to present the past "as it must have been." He is taking history into the world of the imagination and in the process creating his own myths by which the lessons of history are made more clear.

At the same time, Findley's research is almost impeccable. He knows the periods of which he writes in depth, and in *The Wars* he actually creates a deeper illusion of authenticity by presenting the story as the product of an intensive reconstruction of events, even to the extent of inventing taped interviews with the survivors who remember Robert, the hero, and his quixotic attempt to rescue a great troop of horses doomed to a pointless death on the western front. But *The Wars* is not merely the product of research, of vestigial records piled one on top of the other. It is a work of the imagination, of literature, and though history, as Auden once said, "cannot help or pardon," literature can offer understanding and compassion. When Clive, the soldier poet in *The Wars*, is asked "Do you think we'll ever be forgiven for what we've done?" ("we" meaning his generation) he answers: "I doubt we'll ever be forgiven. All I hope is — they'll remember we were human beings."

Famous Last Words is a novel of elaborate artifice, in which fictional figures mingle with people who actually lived and were famous and yet played such artificial roles that they have become as manipulable as the puppets of the imagination. The narrator is actually an offspring of the mind of one of the characters, for Ezra Pound — who appears in the novel in one of his fascistic rages — invented Hugh Selwyn Mauberley, the narrator of *Famous Last Words*, as a minor figure in one of his poems. A fugitive collaborationist at the end of the war in a deserted Alpine hotel, Mauberley writes on the walls and ceilings the story of the bizarre plots in which he and his associates, including the Duke of Windsor and Mrs. Simpson, sought to make use of fascism for their own ends and merely become more deeply mired. Aestheticism and fascism, the lessons seem to read, led to the same dead end. Yet finally, as a manifestation of the urge to live that lies at the heart of even the most extreme aestheticism there is Mauberley's own remark, as he remembers the caves of Altamire and reproduces their smoke-ringed handprint above his own engraved message: "Some there are who never disappear. And I knew I was sitting at the heart of the human race — which is its will to say *I am*." In such a neo-Cartesian statement — which echoes that of Clive in *The Wars* — style becomes its own morality, and understanding assumes more importance than help or pardon.

Not Wanted on the Voyage slips over into fable, taking us far from the world of modern war and politics back to genesis and the world before history. It is the story — retold from a gnostic viewpoint — of the Flood and the voyage of the Ark, seen largely through the eyes of humbler creatures, such as Mottyl the Cat.

Yahweh is presented — like The Old Testament Jehovah by the Gnostics — as a crude and cruel tyrant, personification of all the evil forces and in no sense creative; his minister Dr. Noyes (Noah) is a vivisecting monster. Present throughout is God's rebel child, the androgynous Lucy-Lucifer who accompanies the voyage and at times ironically intervenes, but perhaps in the end the most obdurate rebel is gin-toping Mrs. Noyes, who realizes that the only true world is that which she and Mottyl hold in memory, the old magical world with its dragons and demons and fairies and orgiasts, and its community between humankind and thinking, talking animals which Yahweh and Dr. Noyes wish to purge and sanitize. When the dove comes back with the olive twig, she makes her own prayer: "She prayed, but not to the absent God. Never, never again to the absent God, but to the absent clouds, she prayed. And to the empty sky. She prayed for rain."

Findley describes his sixth novel, *The Telling of Lies*, as "a mystery," and indeed it is so in the double sense that a crime is committed and we have to know the criminal, but at the same time we have to judge the victim and the crime, which in itself is a judgement.

The scene is an old hotel on the Maine coast where a group of American and Canadian patrician families have been wintering for a couple of generations. As Nessa Van Horne, photographer and landscape architect, walks on the beach early one morning, she sees an iceberg that has floated overnight into the bay; it will remain through the novel as a portentous symbol of the indifference of nature. Later in the day, on the beach before the hotel, an ancient billionaire dies mysteriously; his empire in pharmaceutical prod-ucts has become so vast that he boasts of owning one half of the world and renting the rest.

It turns out that the authorities are less than anxious to find the murderer or bring the case to court, particularly as the killing was done — with a tube of poisoned sun lotion — by the wife of a man who had been turned into a human vegetable by the experimental use of Maddox's medicaments. So nobody is brought to justice, but *The Telling of Lies* does not lie entirely in the detective element, which is a slow revealing of the obvious, or in the sombre moral, but as much in the acuity with which personal relations within a limited social class are portrayed and in the atmospheric luminosity with which the beach and its life are evoked, almost like Boudin in prose. Indeed, a good definition of Findley would be atmospheric realist. His plots are rarely plausible, his highly plausible detail is often used for *trompe-l'oeil* illusion, but his atmospheres are always true.

NOTES

¹ "Initram," in *Ladies and Escorts* (Ottawa: Oberon, 1977), p. 88.

² Laurence Mathews, "Norman Levine and His Works," in *Canadian Writers and Their Works*, ed. Robert Lecker, Jack David, and Ellen Quigley, Fiction ser., VIII (Toronto: ECW, 1989), p. 88; hereafter cited as *CWTW*.

³ Norman Levine, *Canada Made Me* (London: Putnam, 1958), p. 255.

⁴ *CWTW*, Fiction ser., VIII, p. 96.

⁵ George Woodcock, "A Saddening Novel of Exile by a Canadian Expatriate," rev. of *From a Seaside Town*, by Norman Levine, *Toronto Daily Star*, 12 Sept. 1970, p. 67.

⁶ "Levine, (Albert) Norman," in *Contemporary Novelists*, 4th ed., ed. D.L. Kirkpatrick (London: St. James, 1986), p. 536.

⁷ Rev. of *Thin Ice*, in *Canadian Book Review Annual 1979*, ed. Dean Tudor, Nancy Tudor, and Kathy Vanderlinden (Toronto: Peter Martin, 1980), p. 167.

⁸ Letter to Edward William Thomson, 29 Aug. 1895, Letter 89, *An Annotated Edition of the Correspondence between Archibald Lampman and Edward William Thomson (1890–1898)*, ed. and introd. Helen Lynn (Ottawa: Tecumseh, 1980), p. 149.

⁹ *CWTW*, Fiction ser., VIII, p. 42.

¹⁰ *CWTW*, Fiction ser., VIII, p. 33.

¹¹ Geoff Hancock, "An Interview with Mavis Gallant," *Canadian Fiction Magazine*, No. 28 (1978) [*A Special Issue on Mavis Gallant*], p. 23.

¹² W.J. Keith, *Canadian Literature in English* (New York: Longman, 1985), p. 157.

¹³ Keith, p. 159.

¹⁴ Geoff Hancock, "An Interview with Leon Rooke," *Canadian Fiction Magazine*, No. 38 (1981), p. 133.

¹⁵ *CWTW*, Fiction ser., VIII, p. 174.

¹⁶ "Leon Rooke," in *Canada Writes: The Members' Book of the Writers Union of Canada*, ed. K.A. Hamilton (Toronto: Writers Union of Canada, 1977), p. 295.

¹⁷ "Audrey Thomas," in *From There to Here: A Guide to English-Canadian*

Literature since 1960 (Erin, Ont.: Porcépic, 1974), p. 254.

[18] *CWTW*, Fiction ser., VIII, p. 199.

[19] Quoted in John Hofsess, "A Teller of Surprising Tales," *The Canadian* [*The Toronto Star*], 6 May 1978, p. 17.

CHAPTER 9

Realism and Neo-Realism: Margaret Laurence, Margaret Atwood, Matt Cohen, Marian Engel, Rudy Wiebe

IN THE MASSIVE SYMPOSIUM ISSUE which in 1984 celebrated the twenty-fifth anniversary of *Canadian Literature*, Matt Cohen wrote an illuminating essay entitled "Notes on Realism in Modern English-Canadian Fiction." In this essay, Cohen notes that in Canada, ". . . the novelistic technique most practised by writers, and most accepted by readers, critics, and academics has been from the beginning and still remains the conventional realistic narrative, though there have been some interesting innovations."[1] Cohen makes it clear that by realism he does not mean the slice-of-life naturalism that once led naïve writers to imagine that in some fairly exact and photographic way they could present what William Godwin, in the subtitle to *Caleb Williams*, called "things as they are." Things as they are, of course, are not even material for history, let alone fiction, since they take a great deal of imaginative shaping and arranging before we see them as not merely actual but in some convincing way "real."

So realism is perhaps based even more than other fictional modes on the illusionist transformation of actuality; verisimilitude in a novel is as much a matter of high skill as it is in the so-called magic realist paintings of Alex Colville or Christopher Pratt, and the best works in the tradition of realist fiction are as far from a literal presentation of life as any work of deliberate fantasy. Matt Cohen remarks: "Realism as a literary movement derives its power from the fact that it goes beyond literature — the making of words and books — to making real the inchoate energies and images that lie in the centre of the imagination" (p. 66). If this is true — and I believe it is — realism overleaps mere mimesis and takes its place under the protection of the muses as a mode that depends on imagination as much as on invention, on creation as much as on observation.

Such imaginative realism offers a place for all the novelists now discussed. In an experimental sense, they are all a great deal more conservative than the best of Canadian short-story writers, among whom the influence of modernism is strongly evident, or than the best of Canadian poets, who have moved into the highly individualized variegation of the post-modernist world. Indeed, one of the novelists in question, Margaret Atwood, offers the example of a prose writer who can be classed as an ironically didactic realist and yet as a verse writer stands among the major post-modernist influences in Canadian poetry.

Cohen — in his brief but important essay — also points out that while, in the classic nineteenth-century realist novels, the characters were "playing out their dreams with each other against a static background," in Canadian novels the climax often occurs when ". . . the characters turn away from each other to re-examine — and re-make — the relationship between themselves and the stage on which the more superficial action of the book is set" (p. 69).

That stage, of course, is the Canadian land, and to the search for the land Canadian writers in general are so exceptionally oriented than even their history tends to be seen in terms of the occupation of the wilderness more than of political change. Politics plays a negligible role in Canadian literature; we have no Trollopes or Disraelis giving it fictional life. Explorers, pioneers, even farmers greatly exceed statesmen in our imaginative life, and for this reason, among others, our fiction, as Cohen points out, has been largely rural-oriented and concerned with coming to terms with "an immense country which overpowers its inhabitants' capacity to hold in their minds the idea of where they live." And the Canadian novelist, he ends by saying with an ironic flip, "must like everyone else try to fill in with his consciousness that most bizarre gap — the lack of a country. This he does by continually re-inventing the country in which his novels would take place — if there were a place for them to take place in" (p. 71).

This kind of search for the land leads many Canadian writers to take peculiar paths to realism. Their physical descriptions of the setting tend to be presented with a heightened authenticity so that, as in Matt Cohen's own imagined community of Salem, somewhere to the north of Kingston, we seem to be moving through the superreal landscape of a dream where actuality is irradiated from within. These settings — so evocatively visualized — tend to be inhabited, as I remark in an essay on Cohen, by "larger-than-life figures caught in situations that resemble those of myth rather than those of real life."[2] Canadian realism — and it is a distinctly local manifestation of the great tradition — merges all the time into myth and fable, using the devices of verisimilitude and illusion, the resources of the mind's eye, to support conceptual structures that with notable intricacy interrelate the objective and the subjective worlds. The realists project, using the clearly delineated setting as a kind of prismatic lens, a powerfully apprehended personal life that Canadians, like primitive peoples, seem unable to detach from the place where it is manifest, the "place to stand on" in Al Purdy's phrase.[3]

Margaret Laurence, who has tended to dominate the fictional landscape of recent decades as Hugh MacLennan dominated it in the 1950s, and who is certainly the most important in the sense of the sheer largeness of her scope among the five novelists now discussed, once said: "Writing, for me, has to be set firmly in some soil, some place, some outer and inner territory which might be described in anthropological terms as 'cultural background.' "[4] And elsewhere, confessing her special attachment to Canada among all the lands where she has lived or travelled, she explains:

This is where my world began. A world which includes the ancestors — both my own and other people's ancestors who become mine. A world which formed me, and continues to do so, even while I fought it in some of its aspects, and continue to do so. A world which gave me my own lifework to do, because it was here that I learned the sight of my own particular eyes.[5]

But Laurence came to writing of her own world, the world that gave her a lifework, by foreign paths, for it was, as J.M. Kertzer remarks, Africa that set her writing: "She found Africa totally alien and strangely familiar. Paradoxically, this exotic milieu allowed her to take a leading place within a Canadian literary tradition."[6] And indeed this apparent contradiction of finding themselves through drinking of foreign springs of inspiration is one of the main ways in which the novelists here discussed are distinguished from earlier Canadian writers. In sentiment they are often more nationalist; in derivation more cosmopolitan, rather like those Indian students who, like Gandhi, left home to gather their liberatory ideas and returned to apply them. As Matt Cohen said to an interviewer: "I think I understand those people who come back better than those who go away."[7]

With odd brilliant exceptions like Sara Jeannette Duncan, who began her literary career in Canada, continued it during a long residence in India, and managed to keep her Canadian fiction completely separate from her Indian novels, Canadian writers of any significance until the later 1950s mainly wrote about Canadian settings and Canadian themes, even when, like Morley Callaghan, they sometimes did so in a language largely modelled on contemporary American sources.

The Prairie novels of Robert J.C. Stead and Martha Ostenso, of W.O. Mitchell and Sinclair Ross, and even of Frederick Philip Grove despite his concealed earlier career as a European writer, were derived almost entirely from experience of life in the great plains of the West, and though the protagonists might be immigrants who had come from abroad with their heavy and inappropriate baggage of ideas and prejudices, their real destinies always worked themselves out in situations dominated by the harsh and demanding natural forces of the Canadian environment. Morley Callaghan's parables, in novel form, of the 1930s were — despite the European experiences he later described in *That Summer in Paris* — wholly Canadian in locality, in social background, and even in imagery. The massive and broadly didactic novels with which Hugh MacLennan largely dominated the Canadian literary scene during the 1950s may have taken their underlying themes from the antique cycles of Odysseus and Oedipus, but they transported them into a setting that in political and cultural terms, with its obsession with the assertion of national independence and the reconciliation of the country's double racial and cultural strains, was entirely Canadian, with little left of British mental domination, and as yet little sensitivity to American intrusion.

These novelists of the period when late colonialism merged into a national consciousness wrote almost entirely of Canadian themes, and whether they did so in the grand and somewhat allegorical manner of Grove's *The Master of the Mill,* or with the much more self-effacing didacticism of MacLennan's *Barometer Rising* or Ross's *As for Me and My House,* they kept their action within Canada and their characters safely Canadian. Indeed, though it was curiously innocent of xenophobia, the period from the early 1930s to the late 1950s may have been the least cosmopolitan in Canadian fiction. This happened not only for literary reasons — because Canadian writers were becoming aware as never before of their immediate physical and social environments and finding in them an abundance of questions, if not of answers, to stimulate their imaginative responses — but also for reasons that were connected with the limited infrastructure of the Canadian literary world at this period. Those few Canadian writers whose books were sighted outside Canada usually published with houses in London or New York, while, conversely, to be issued in Canada at that period, a novel had to be locally oriented in the obvious kind of way that would give the Toronto publishers — who mostly made their livings distributing foreign books under the agency system — a little patriotic justification.

One can seldom give a single reason for any major shift in a cultural landscape. Experiential patterns change, as they did a few years after the end of World War II, when a variety of reasons led numbers of young Canadians to live in formerly colonial countries in circumstances different from those of their predecessors who had gone there as colonial servants. Literary influences shifted as the simple colonial-national pattern that sustained Canadian writers in the 1930s and 1940s became complicated by cosmopolitan influences coming strongly in from elsewhere in the American continent, from Europe, and eventually from Asia. The infrastructure of the literary world started to change in the 1960s as magazines multiplied and native publishers concerned mainly with producing Canadian books began to emerge parallel to the old branch-plant houses and the agency houses; both Margaret Atwood and Matt Cohen played active roles in this development. And during the 1960s a series of movements tangential to the main culture — the student revolt, feminism, environmentalism, nationalism, the mystique of participatory democracy, and the antiwar movement in its successive phases — all affected Canadian writers in various ways, though, with a good sense of artistic self-preservation, very few of them became involved in a partisan manner. This does not mean that their writing was unaffected, and the five novelists discussed in this volume were among those most sensitive to such trends of their times.

In chronological terms, they are a fairly closely contained group — the eldest, Margaret Laurence, being only sixteen years older than the youngest, Matt Cohen — and their first novels appeared in an even shorter span, between 1960, when Margaret Laurence's *This Side Jordan* was published, and 1969, when both Margaret Atwood's *The Edible Woman* and Matt Cohen's *Korsoniloff* came off the press. The cosmopolitan influences of the time were reinforced for all of them by experience. Margaret Laurence in Somaliland and Ghana and Marian Engel in Cyprus were witnesses to the transitions from colonial to postcolonial societies, transitions that in important ways meant the resurgence of older, preimperial traditions rather than the entry into brave new worlds of liberation. Marian Engel and Rudy Wiebe both studied in Europe, while Matt Cohen took the French writer Albert Camus as the subject for his Master's thesis. Atwood and Wiebe spent periods in American academies, and it was during a long residence in England that Margaret Laurence developed, out of memory and imagination, the mythical town of Manawaka and worked her first Canadian novels into its patterns of life. Sooner or later, all except one of the five writers felt the challenge to write novels set in countries other than Canada: Margaret Laurence at the beginning of her career in *This Side Jordan*, Marian Engel mid-way with *Monodromos*, and Margaret Atwood and Matt Cohen with novels, which are among their best — Cohen's *The Spanish Doctor*, set in renaissance Europe and later *Nadine*, and Atwood's *Bodily Harm*, dominated by political events on a Caribbean island which uncannily anticipated actual happenings a little while later in Grenada. And even Rudy Wiebe's most complex novel, *The Blue Mountains of China*, is a kind of epic of Mennonite history, set largely in Russia, China, and Paraguay, and his other two considerable works, *The Temptations of Big Bear* and *The Scorched-Wood People*, concern cultures that were exotic in terms of his own Mennonite background and indeed in terms of the backgrounds of average Canadians, whether WASP or Québécois.

There is a way in which one can call these five writers, and perhaps two or three more of the same generation, the first real all-Canadian novelists, in the sense that they did not feel obliged to be self-conscious about their Canadianism in the same way as Hugh MacLennan during the period when he seemed set on presenting in fiction all our concerns as social beings living in the northern half of North America. These writers have not only lived and studied and written abroad, and at times taken foreign places as the settings for their novels, they have also profited from the study of foreign novelists and, consciously or unconsciously, recognized their affinities with them. Matt Cohen's first small book, *Korsoniloff*, was in spirit, and even in form, nearer to French *nouvelle vague* fiction than to anything being written in Canada at that time, and Marian Engel's novels, as I once remarked, can best be fitted into the French category of the *récit*, which Camus and Gide applied to most of their medium-length fictions, for they are "simple, patterned, stylized, moralist, as the masterpieces of minor French fiction have been in our time."[8] And yet, with all this openness to alien experience and these resemblances to foreign analogues, it would be hard to find a group of novelists who, thanks largely to their liberation from *self-conscious* Canadianism, have more remarkably projected the inner reality of Canadian life. MacLennan's very didactic presentation of Canadian problems in his novels, all the way from *Barometer Rising* to *Return of the Sphinx*, was, as I have said, dominated by the use of alien myths from Greek antiquity that he had absorbed during his first career as a classical historian; Callaghan also, in his postwar novels, became obsessed with the simulacrum of an antique myth, that of lost Eurydice. But, despite the openness that some of the novelists we are considering have shown to certain international developments in the technique of fiction, they have also shown a determination to develop native, rather than to use alien, myths, and here, I suggest, lies the success of their adaptations of realism.

At least two mythical communities, Margaret Laurence's Mana-waka and Matt Cohen's Salem, with their own invented histories, have risen in the mind's eye within recognizable Canadian settings. Canadian landscapes, insular ones in each case, form the stages for the quasi-mythical encounters of Margaret Atwood's *Surfacing* and Marian Engel's *Bear*, which show human beings — women in both cases — reaching self-integration through an encounter with natural forces whose manifestations resemble native animist initiation. In her Manawaka cycle, Margaret Laurence uses the ancient doctrine of the four elements and their corresponding humours to illuminate in mythical terms the life journeys towards self-knowledge of four women of widely various types. Hagar the earth-bound in *The Stone Angel*, Stacey the fire-threatened in *The Fire-Dwellers*, the airily insubstantial Rachel in *A Jest of God*, and fluid Morag in *The Diviners* present an elemental pattern of Canadian life in all its aspects, in which, in the final novel, the reconciliation comes through the relationships of Morag (water) with her three lovers, the evasive Brooke Skelton (air), the earthy painter of rocks Dan McRaith, and the fiery Métis Jules Tonnerre, whose own sister was burned to death in the kind of combustion that Stacey MacAindra feared for herself and her children. Fire and water coming together to produce the ultimate reconciliation of the elements are shown in the child, Piquette, born of the union of Morag and Jules, the novelist and the singer, the two truly creative beings in Margaret Laurence's vast gallery of characterizations. Both Matt Cohen in *Wooden Hunters* and Rudy Wiebe in *The Temptations of Big Bear* use the memory of native myths to illuminate the contrast between aboriginal ways of living in and off the land and modern ways of dominating the land, to the eventual destruction of human and natural orders.

In the process of making it a vehicle of myth, these novelists have liberated realism from its slavery to representationalism, to mimesis, to the urge to show things as they are. They have used plausibility, as great fabulists like Jonathan Swift and George Orwell did, to make the improbable authentic, and so have broadened the area of imaginative expression. They have provided means by which fiction could be used, without seeming gauchely didactic, to illuminate the moral, and even the political, concerns of modern human beings and to illuminate history with the light of the imagination rather than with the flickering candle of conjecture. And they have found an approach that allows each of them not only to develop within the realist frame special visions and a particular view of the times to which the novelist belongs, but also to apply her or his special literary strengths to the tasks undertaken. Margaret Laurence's strengths, for example, are her power of evocative visualization and her sense of character as being the central factor in fiction. "For Laurence," as J.M. Kertzer remarks, "novelists require, first, a good eye, but second, an imaginative sympathy allowing them to enter into the personalities of their characters."[9] In placing her emphasis on characterization, she stepped aside from radical experimentation and turned to early modern "psychological" novelists like Henry James as the models whose conventions she "adopted, polished, and made her own." Kertzer, who is illuminating on Laurence's fictional technique, goes on to tell us:

> Laurence calls this form the "Method novel," after the exam-ple of method acting: the author inhabits his or her characters and takes on their personalities. She contrasts her method with the broader social realism of Hugh MacLennan, Morley Callaghan, Ernest Buckler, and Sinclair Ross, an earlier generation of novelists who analyzed "the whole social pattern."[10]

Laurence's novels are centred on a series of striking individuals, and if they are not strictly *Bildungsromane*, tracing the develop-ment of the central figure from youth to maturity, they resemble them to the extent that they show the central characters at some crucial time in their lives coming to terms with their pasts and in doing so moving out of ignorance and indecision into awareness and self-confidence. Sometimes the moment of self-recognition comes at the end, as it reaches Hagar Shipley a brief time before death, and sometimes it comes when there is life ahead in which to apply it, as happens to Rachel Cameron in *A Jest of God*, but whenever it does arrive, it brings, not an assurance of happiness, but a possibility of serenity unknown before. Since so much in such a presentation depends on our understanding the point of view from which the story is told, the narrative voice — as many critics have followed Laurence herself in pointing out — is of crucial importance in her writing, and Laurence in fact prefers to talk of her "voice" rather than her "style," though in fact the sheer genius with which she hears and reproduces the voices of her characters becomes her style. Her novels are not only, as she likes to think them, well made; they are also, which is perhaps an inevitable condition of good making, superbly well told.

However, while Laurence's beginning is the character who takes up residence in her mind, and while she aims at "the whole exploration of personality,"[11] it is perhaps misleading to say, as Kertzer does, that ". . . social concerns, while never absent from her novels, appear only as they impinge on individual lives." This would seem to suggest that the society appears merely as background to the lives of the characters, but in fact Manawaka as a community, and other Canadian places like Vancouver and southern Ontario, do take on collective character, so that, as well as fully recollected individual lives, we are presented also with ways-of-life and social structures that are equally well realized, though the fact that they are seen often through the lens of shaping memory means that we see them in mythical, rather than actual, dimensions. And within these little worlds of small town or suburbs are worked out the themes for which Laurence has been impelled to find appropriate forms, themes that Kertzer rightly lists as "freedom, survival, colonialism (or forms of coercion), and the plight of women."[12]

There is a peculiar spaciousness to Margaret Laurence's novels that is closely linked to her empathy for the broad prairie landscapes in which she was reared, a spaciousness that once tempted me to compare her with Tolstoy, in terms of kind rather than greatness: he as the novelist of the steppes, she as the novelist of the great North American plains. As I remarked: ". . . there is a particular closeness between them in the fact that each is seeking to deal with a land of exceptional vastness, and also to reconcile a sense of history in a time of rapid change . . . with a passionate sense of the importance of personal experiences and particular destinies."[13]

If I were continuing this kind of comparison between Canadian and Russian writers, it would be Turgenev rather than Tolstoy whom I would compare with Marian Engel, for he, like she, has a kind of empathetic relationship with the tradition of French realism that derived from Flaubert. Such comparisons are not inappropriate in connection with Marian Engel, for though she was extremely active in the Canadian literary world, defending the interests of writers and seeking to elevate their position in public consideration, any kind of literary nationalism — in the sense of seeing Canadian fiction as detached from international trends — would be quite remote from her outlook. As Elizabeth Brady justly remarks:

> For Marian Engel, the world of ideas was a constant transgressor of national boundaries: the practice of writing novels — and literary criticism — in terms of national categories was as alien to her as would be the shelving of library books according to class, race, or gender.[14]

Ideas, including ideas about gender, play an important role in Marian Engel's novels. But one of the most interesting features of her writing is the way in which ideas are made not only to motivate credible human beings but also to become manifest in settings described with a visual meticulousness that in its more virtuoso instances, as in the rich and elaborate descriptions of Cypriot towns and landscapes in *Monodromos*, reminds one of the luminous and detailed painting of the Pre-Raphaelite Brotherhood. Ideas, like people, in her books, need places to inhabit, and, just as much as Margaret Laurence, she is a creator of vividly apprehended imaginative landscapes, presented with the accurate economy of a practised miniaturist. Her extraordinary control of prose enables her to attain this economy of means and effect, so that her best books are short books, all the more intense for their condensation.

With such talents, Marian Engel was peculiarly fitted to adopt, in *Bear*, that special offshoot of realism, the fable, where the plausibility of the setting authenticates the action, however improbable, and deepens the underlying message (for didacticism is a necessary feature of the genre). *Bear*, indeed, is perhaps mostly distinguished by its curiously transparent objectivity, which, as I once said, makes ". . . the earthy and the fantastic dance in proper harmony."[15]

Bear, of course, was largely a *succès de scandale* for reasons which Marian Engel had not intended; it was also, and more importantly, a technical triumph that led some critics to see it almost in isolation, as if Engel were virtually a "one-book" novelist. In fact, she is a writer of great versatility. Her novels do not echo each other except in the rather general matter of the gender of her central figures, who are all women. The tight *récit* of *The Honeyman Festival*, the descriptive evocation of place and history in *Monodromos*, the fable of *Bear*, are different kinds of novels, and so, from all the others, is *The Glassy Sea*, with its epistolary core that reminds one of early English women novelists like Aphra Behn and Mary Manley. Yet there are links, of style and idea, among all these books, and *The Glassy Sea* really complements *Bear* in the sense of going back to the double basic nature of man, so that where *Bear* seeks a recognition of the animal within us, *The Glassy Sea* pleads the acceptance that we are angelic also. *Bear* is a fable of reconciliation with the natural world to which by origin we belong; *The Glassy Sea* is a psychological novel about the search for the spiritual perfection to which we aspire and the strange ways in which we often find it. What really unites these novels is the eloquent and accurate prose, in which every word tells and adds, and which made Marian Engel one of the finest stylists to have used Canadian English.

Perhaps confusing realism, with its broad scope of techniques and approaches, with Zolaesque naturalism, Rudy Wiebe has resisted critical attempts to classify him as a realist. And indeed it is true that in his novels there is what William H. New in *Literary History of Canada* has dryly described as "a certain artificiality of structure"[16] and Sam Solecki in *The Oxford Companion to Canadian Literature* has praised as an experimentalism "in style and form."[17] Solecki even asserts that Wiebe's major novels are "among our most successful experimental works,"[18] though in this area one cannot seriously compare them with *The Double Hook* or *Beautiful Losers* or the fiction of John Metcalf and Clark Blaise.

In the same way, I think we have to modify Susan Whaley's statement that "Rudy Wiebe's art is neither Christian, nor ethnic, nor regional, although each of these concerns certainly informs his work."[19] It is always hard, in fact, to detach a work of art from the spirit that informs it, since without that spirit, it might not even have come into being. An African sculpture is dependent for its very origination on the animism that inspires it; a structure like the cathedral in Chartres, or even the great sculptures that form part of its fabric, could not exist without the presence of a church and a faith to provide the impulse to build it. In this sense, the sculpture *is* animist, the cathedral *is* Christian. And in the same way, Rudy Wiebe's novels *are* Christian *and* ethnic *and* regional. His first three novels would not have been written as they are had he not been born a Mennonite and continued, as Whaley remarks, to see himself as "a radical follower of the person of Jesus Christ."[20] It was his own ethnicity, in the sense of being aware of belonging to a community apart from, and largely rejected by, the rest of Canadian society, that led him into novels that are advocacies, as well as mythical histories, of other communities apart, like the Indians and the Métis. And though important parts of *The Blue Mountains of China* take place outside Canada, the corpus of Wiebe's work is Western Canadian in its inspiration and in its view of the world, which is not to say that it is *only* regionalist. For the most universal of novels are so because of the depth of their roots in a particular setting. The paradox of all art — and indeed of all science — is that in observing the particular with attention we evoke the universal.

This is what Wiebe does, and it is his strength. It has enabled him to give a peculiar kind of historical solidity to his writings that comes from his special sense of local tradition. "What we have to do," Susan Whaley quotes him as saying, "is dig up the whole tradition, not just the white one. It's not a recorded tradition, it's a verbal one."[21] The hearsay narratives passed on among Mennonites and Indians and Métis become woven into the substance of his novels, and here his work is in appearance vastly different from that of Margaret Laurence, the other notable novelist of the Canadian prairie, in that where each of her novels talks in a single voice, that of the protagonist directly or indirectly, Wiebe will use several narrative voices, as he does most successfully in *The Blue Mountains of China*, which I regard as his best novel up to the present. It is so, I think, because here he has best balanced his powerful command of symbol and language with his didactic inclinations. When his didactic inclinations overbalanced his aesthetic ones, the equilibrium was lost, as happened in his novel about the Métis rebellions, *The Scorched-Wood People.* I still stand by the opinion I expressed on that book at the time of its publication: that, in writing it, Wiebe has been unable "to separate the purpose of historical fiction, which is to give us a plausible image and feeling of the past, from that of the historical moralist, which is to apportion blame, signal merit and formulate lessons."[22]

Historical writing is bound up with the sense of time. But in fiction, time can find expression in two ways — as a simulated objective record, usually delivered in the third person, and as memory, usually delivered in the first person. The classic historical novel tended to follow time chronologically, as to this day does the work of some of its best exponents, like Mary Renault; realistic fiction since Proust has tended to adopt the nonchronological patterns of memory, so that time becomes as much part of the present as it is of the past, and projects events in a shifting light of recession and proximity. It is almost a prerequisite of the modern novel that, unlike the short story which can stand in the immediate present, it should find its own special, nonchronological way to deal with time.

Laurence's Hagar Shipley in *The Stone Angel* and Stacey MacAindra in *The Fire Dwellers* live in interior monologues where memory creates an erratic, yet seamless, continuum. In Marian Engel's *The Honeyman Festival*, action and place observe the classic unities — a single house where everything takes place in twelve hours — but time expands on the associations created by those small events of social intercourse that occur in that short duration within that small space.

Matt Cohen, perhaps, deals with time in the most varied ways. After his earlier and highly experimental novellas and short stories, of which *Korsoniloff* and *Johnny Crackle Sings* were most typical, he proceeded between 1974 and 1981 to a more conventional series of novels about rural Canada. They can be linked with the more obviously experimental novels because they work less by linear chronology than by a constant interpenetration of past and present. In all of them, *The Disinherited* (1974), *Wooden Hunters* (1975), *The Colours of War* (1977), *The Sweet Second Summer of Kitty Malone* (1979), and *Flowers of Darkness* (1981), there is a disturbing sense of the provisional in the lives of all their characters, and ominous transitions that do not always turn out to be disastrous. Except for *Wooden Hunters*, which takes place among deprived Indians and washed-up whites on an island representing one of the Queen Charlottes, all these novels are set in the environs of the fictional town of Salem in the southern Ontario countryside.

The Disinherited is a kind of family chronicle in which the last illness of Richard Thomas takes us back, by way of the ramblings and recollections of his hospitalized mind, through the four generations of family that settled the Upper Canadian wilderness, created a flourishing farm, and, in the successive conflicts between fathers and sons, has seen a whole social order — that of the Ontario farmlands — arise and decay within a century.

Cohen tends, especially in *The Colours of War*, to use time and memory to reveal social patterns in relation to individual development. The novel, ostensibly about a future civil war in Canada, is also an observation of the way in which, in difficult times, men tend to turn to the past as a refuge, as Theodore Beam, in a disintegrating society, sets out for his home of Salem with its solid-stone-walled houses, and once there, slips further into the past by living, in a war-torn and terrorized society, off the land like a primitive man. *The Sweet Second Summer of Kitty Malone* centres on two ugly, lifeworn people living in the environs of Salem, and gains its effect from inverting the pattern of the customary romance. *Flowers of Darkness*, which shows the destruction of a demonic preacher in Salem by the consequences of his own hypocrisy, reads in many ways like a genial parody of William Faulkner, to whose Yoknapatawpha County, Cohen's own country of the imagination, Salem, has been compared.

This combination of the subjective approach to time through memory with the more objective approach to it through the life of human collectivities led Cohen to depart even from the decayed present of Salem and to attempt a revival of the historical novels. Travelling in Europe, Cohen became for the first time absorbed in his Jewish past, and in the early 1980s, adopting the spirit of high parody, he wrote *The Spanish Doctor* looking back five hundred years and reconstructing in a splendidly realized chronological setting the life of the surgeon, intellectual, and Jew, Avram Halevi, who in 14th and early 15th century Europe rebels against the norms of his era.

Cohen has spent much time recently in France, and his most recent novels, *Nadine* and *Emotional Arithmetic*, concern the experience of Jews in that country during the period of German occupation, when those who lived in Paris were rounded up and shipped to a camp in the suburb of Drancy which became a way station for Auschwitz. They are, in their way, books about the

Holocaust, but they are not books of despair; rather, they are books about the triumph of the human will and spirit. Just as Avram Helavy, the hero of *The Spanish Doctor*, finds his way through a great series of scrapes in the manner of Dumas' heroes and eventually makes his way to Kief to die of old age, so the central figures of *Emotional Arithmetic* pass through the fears and trials of the camps and escape as wise and compassionate human beings to plot the release of other victims.

These are fine books about living on the edge of disaster and surviving. The perils are realistically, even melodramatically revealed. But the powers of human will and love are never lost and so we are led to serene, credible and satisfying solutions. It is a rare achievement, to write a happy ending — transforming tragedy into benign comedy — that is neither mawkish nor implausible, but Cohen has done it more than once.

Margaret Atwood stands apart in this group of novelists because she is also a poet of unusual power and sensitivity. Early in this essay I defined her as "an ironically didactic realist," meaning that to apply to her fiction, but I also said, in an essay I wrote on her some years ago, that "no other writer in Canada of Margaret Atwood's generation has so wide a command of the resources of literature, so telling a restraint in their use."[23] The restraint is, of course, particularly evident in her extraordinarily condensed and pointed poetry; the wide command is there in her fiction, where she appears as a veritable *magistra ludi*, conducting the games of literature with exemplary versatility.

Her absorption of the Gothic strain, to which she devoted her academic studies, into her fiction has been noted by a number of critics. It is used, of course, with notably parodic effect in *Lady Oracle*, but, subtly combined with a knowledge of Jungian psychology and an awareness of animist beliefs, it provides the impetus for *Surfacing*, which remains one of her best works in fiction.

But the Gothic is only one element in her fiction, though it is an important one, since it creates a vital tension between the ritual, and therefore implausible, nature of much that takes place in her novels (the creation and consumption of the edible woman in the book that bears her name, the regression to the primitive in the narrator of *Surfacing*, the faked death of the heroine in *Lady Oracle*) and the plausibility of the narrative style. Her novels are also social, criticizing the false elements in our own society, exposing the cruelties elsewhere of which Atwood in acutely conscious; it would be difficult to justify detaching what happens in *Bodily Harm* from its author's personal involvement in Amnesty International. And though a strain of sheer playfulness, of mocking her readers as well as her characters, often appears in Atwood's novels, that is really surface play. Beneath, there is always a serious intent and a threat perceived. As Ildikó de Papp Carrington so accurately says:

> Every novel is tightly organized through an obsessive metaphorical network to dramatize her protagonists' developing consciousness. Although they see themselves menaced by external enemies, they repeatedly discover the same enemy within.
>
> . . . .
> What survives is stubbornly innate human evil: the demon within.[24]

There has, in Atwood's most recent novels, been a perceptible tightening of the realistic structure, and a corresponding turn towards a pessimistic view of human nature, human destiny. As Carrington points out, ". . . *Life Before Man* is not about the discovery of identity, but about its loss," and the same applies to *Bodily Harm*, where the demons are objectified; they are at large, not only within the individual consciousness, but even more menacingly in the world outside. It is this revelation that our fears and actuality are ultimately the same that surely makes Atwood our most knowing and complete realist.

The versatility of her approaches has been shown in her most recent novels, *The Handmaid's Tale*, certainly her most controversial, and *Cat's Eye*, arguably her best. *The Handmaid's Tale* is a futurist story, a dystopia with a twist, since the future Atwood envisages turns resolutely towards the past in the Republic of Gilead not too many years ahead. There all the hopes of contemporary religious fundamentalists are realized in a society where the family is sanctified, and in the name of Christianity women will take the kind of place Hitler once allotted to them, attending the kitchen and cradle. Satire in *The Handmaid's Tale* is expressed in the deadpan descriptiveness with which the absurd rules and customs of Gilead are shown in action. But it is the absence of credible human conflict that mars *The Handmaid's Tale*, like many other futurist fictions, and the novel, which leaves a repellance in the mind, can best be considered an ingenious but tentative exercise by a versatile writer.

Cat's Eye, which appeared in 1988, is Atwood's most complex and most fully realized novel. It might have, for an epigraph, Graham Greene's adaptation of Wordsworth's phrase, "Hell lies around us in our infancy," for it is inspired by views of childhood as dark as Original Sin itself. Small girls, as Atwood presents them, are cruel, evil-minded little monsters, as eager to fasten on a temperamentally weaker child as piranhas to attack a wounded member of their own species. In *Cat's Eye* the painter Elaine Risley, who has long lived on the West Coast, returns to Toronto for a retrospective exhibition, and as she walks the streets of her old home city she remembers the dark hours but also the bright days of her childhood, particularly in the wild regions where her father's profession as an entomologist drew the family, so that her memory is not all shadow but dappled like most of our pasts. There is comedy as well as cruelty in Elaine's relationship with her chief tormentor, Cordelia, and throughout the novel the ambivalence of human feelings and relationships is woven into a pattern of compassion and sharp honest insight as by returning to the scenes of pain Elaine exorcizes the past. It is said that criminals return to the scene of the crime; so do victims, Atwood suggests, and perhaps more effectively.

NOTES

[1] Matt Cohen, "Notes on Realism in Modern English-Canadian Fiction," *Canadian Literature*, No. 100 (Spring 1984), p. 65. All further references to this work appear in the text.

[2] George Woodcock, "Matt Cohen and His Works," in *Canadian Writers and Their Works*, ed. Robert Lecker, Jack David, and Ellen Quigley, Fiction ser., IX (Toronto: ECW, 1987), p. 136; hereafter cited as *CWTW*.

[3] Al Purdy, "Roblin's Mills (2)," in *Selected Poems* (Toronto: McClelland and Stewart, 1972), p. 117.

[4] Margaret Laurence, "Sources," *Mosaic*, 3, No. 3 (Spring 1970), 80–84; rpt. (rev.) "A Place to Stand On," in *Heart of a Stranger* (Toronto: McClelland and Stewart, 1976), pp. 17–18.

5 Margaret Laurence, "Where the World Began," *Maclean's*, Dec. 1972, pp. 23, 80; rpt. (rev.) in *Heart of a Stranger*, p. 219.

6 *CWTW*, Fiction ser., IX, p. 257.

7 Alan Twigg, "Matt Cohen: Eastern Horizon," in *For Openers: Conversations with Twenty-Four Canadian Writers* (Madeira Park, B.C.: Harbour, 1981), p. 181.

8 George Woodcock, "Casting Down Their Golden Crowns: The Novels of Marian Engel," in *The Human Elements: Second Series*, ed. David Helwig (Ottawa: Oberon, 1981), p. 11.

9 *CWTW*, Fiction ser., IX, p. 258.

10 *CWTW*, Fiction ser., IX, p. 261.

11 Donald Cameron, "Margaret Laurence: The Black Celt Speaks of Freedom," in *Conversations with Canadian Novelists* (Toronto: Macmillan, 1973), Pt. 1, p. 104.

12 *CWTW*, Fiction ser., IX, p. 260.

13 George Woodcock, "The Human Elements: Margaret Laurence's Fiction," in *The Human Elements: Critical Essays*, ed. David Helwig (Ottawa: Oberon, 1978), pp. 134–61; rpt. in *The World of Canadian Writing: Critiques and Recollections* (Vancouver: Douglas & McIntyre, 1980), p. 41.

14 *CWTW*, Fiction ser., IX, p. 184.

15 Woodcock, "Casting Down Their Golden Crowns," p. 32.

16 William H. New, "Fiction," in *Literary History of Canada: Canadian Literature in English*, 2nd ed., gen. ed. and introd. Carl F. Klinck (Toronto: Univ. of Toronto Press, 1976), III, 247.

17 Sam Solecki, "Rudy Wiebe," in *The Oxford Companion to Canadian Literature*, ed. William Toye (Toronto: Oxford Univ. Press, 1983), p. 829.

18 Solecki, p. 829.

19 *CWTW*, Fiction ser., IX, p. 316.

20 Donald Cameron, "Rudy Wiebe: The Moving Stream Is Perfectly at Rest," in *Conversations with Canadian Novelists*, p. 148.

21 George Melnyk, "The Western Canadian Imagination: An Interview with Rudy Wiebe," *Canadian Fiction Magazine*, No. 12 (Winter 1974), p. 32

22 George Woodcock, "Riel and Dumont," rev. of *The Scorched-Wood People*, *Canadian Literature*, No. 77 (Summer 1978), p. 99.

23 George Woodcock, "Margaret Atwood: Poet as Novelist," in *The Canadian Novel in the Twentieth Century: Essays from Canadian Literature*, ed. George Woodcock, New Canadian Library, No. 115 (Toronto: McClelland and Stewart, 1975), p. 327.

24 *CWTW*, Fiction ser., IX, pp. 39, 41.

CHAPTER 10

Fiction and Metafiction:
Leonard Cohen, Dave Godfrey,
Robert Kroetsch, Robert Harlow,
Jack Hodgins

IN AN EXCELLENT ESSAY on Leonard Cohen as novelist, Linda Hutcheon confronts boldly the question of defining the kind of novels, uncomfortably self-conscious, unashamedly artificial, which the five novelists now under consideration for the most part offer us. Proceeding from Cohen's early *Künstlerroman, The Favourite Game*, to his second and more celebrated novel, *Beautiful Losers*, she makes a statement that should not be allowed to drop out of one's mind in considering not only Cohen, but also Dave Godfrey, Robert Kroetsch, Robert Harlow, and, to an extent at least, Jack Hodgins:

> *Beautiful Losers* is, if anything, even more self-consciously aware of the artist as persona in relation to the process of creation. But it is more in the form than in the thematized content of the novel that is manifest the auto-referential nature of what today is being called metafiction, fiction about fiction, fiction that contains within itself a first critical commentary on its own narrative or linguistic identity. Although some writers and critics today want to call this kind of novel "postmodernist," the obvious literary, historical, and logical implications of such terminology seem to create more problems than such a coining solves. The more descriptive term, *metafiction*, is more cautious and will be used here for that reason.[1]

Hutcheon's caution is entirely praiseworthy, for though the writers here discussed have been termed postmodernist by some of their critics, and at times seem to have accepted the label, the fact remains that metafictional elements in their work, which are held to justify the assumption of their postmodernism, find premonitory echoes in works written and published generations, centuries, even millennia ago.

Most of the elements of what we now talk of as postmodernism exist already in the highly artificial and self-conscious metafiction of that founding modernist, Wyndham Lewis. But we can go much farther back than Lewis, to Laurence Sterne and the great literary fame of *Tristam Shandy*, to the spate of prose mock epics that, following Pope's verse parody of the genre, *The Rape of the Lock*, were produced by English eighteenth-century novelists, and beyond them to the sixteenth- and seventeenth-century models of such books: *Don Quixote*, that *tour de force* literary mirror work, everlastingly mingling the process of storytelling with the story; and *Gargantua and Pantagruel*, the Rabelaisian masterpiece of burlesque to which Hutcheon quite appropriately relates *Beautiful Losers*. We could even go back to the Hellenistic pastiches of the Homeric epics and to the parodic comedy of Aristophanes. Ever since rhapsodes became writers and set their epics down on papyrus, the temptation of the palimpsest has always been there: to improve on the basic text, to rewrite life and so subsume it into the work of art, and to make the reader a member of this literary conspiracy.

Perhaps more than in any other of the writers here discussed, we see the reflections of this metafictional past in Cohen. For clearly — in the black romanticism that has been justly attributed to him — he goes back to the most important recent source of the theory and practice of literature as artefact that we have, the Decadence. The aestheticist reconstruction of reality that is one of the most important elements in *Beautiful Losers* relates Cohen's work not only to the practice of decadent writers like Baudelaire and Huysmans, Beardsley and Wilde, but also to the artistic theories of the movement, and especially to the idea — which Northrop Frye, with less than ample acknowledgements, borrowed from Wilde and naturalized in North American academia — that all art, including literature, really derives from other art, and that our perceptions of life are inevitably conditioned by our experience of art or of whatever in our special time and place is its surrogate.

Cohen fits into this pattern on two levels. First, there is his highly technical approach to the art of fiction, which resembles much more that of a poet than that of a storyteller. As Hutcheon points out, "Like many other Canadian poets — Margaret Atwood, George Bowering, Gwendolyn MacEwen — Cohen has turned to the formal resources of verse in order to develop new novelistic techniques within a tradition of fiction that is predominantly realistic."[2] On the one hand, this tendency is manifest in Cohen's desire not only to play the game of literature, of parody and palimpsest, but also to involve his audience, so that what he seeks, even if he does not achieve it with every reader, is a kind of partnership, a participation in the great and often sardonic jest that what we are reading in *Beautiful Losers* is not meant as a representation of life, and indeed is not in any real sense *about* life, but rather about the artistic transformation of life, just as his earlier novel, *The Favourite Game*, was less concerned with the loves of the hero, who was in any case most happy loving himself, than with his development as an artist relating all experience to his own creativity. As Hutcheon justly remarks, "From his songs to his books, all of Cohen's work revolves around his own personality as an artist, his 'life in art.' "[3]

But when one's life is in art, art by reversion becomes the substance of one's life, and one's interpretations of the process of living tend to become fabricated out of a cultural detritus that need not be made up entirely from abandoned high art. And here we reach the great ambivalence — or apparent ambivalence — within Cohen's work. On the one side, there is the sophisticated and quasi-aestheticist use of palimpsest and parody as structural factors, so that *Beautiful Losers* not only abounds in literary echoes but also burlesques historical and religious texts and pornographic fiction; as Cohen himself remarks, it also uses for its own purposes and in its own ways the "conventional techniques of pornographic suspense, of humour, of plot, or character development and conventional intrigues."[4] On the other side, there is the use of pop culture — comic books, movies, and popular music — a practice of Cohen's that Hutcheon gives a kind of quasi-political intent when she remarks, "This culture is obviously set in opposition to the official culture of the eternal and the serious . . . ," and when she adds, "Literature, to Cohen, must be opened up to the energy of the people."[5]

I would suggest that here the utilization of pop culture, which has helped to shape Cohen's self-image as an artist, is being mistakenly equated with the development of populist sentiment. There is little evidence in Cohen's writing that he cares for the people, either collectively or as individuals. But pop culture is a totally different matter, since it is another way of creating art out of artefact, of using the commercialized mass entertainment which is today's "opium of the people" to fabricate works which are beyond the people's understanding. Cohen's songs undoubtedly have had a certain popular following, but to see a piece of literary *esoterica* like *Beautiful Losers* as inspired by "the energy of the people" is no more reasonable than it would be to see *The Picture of Dorian Gray*, with its lurid vignettes of East London low life, as a proletarian masterpiece. In both cases, the life of the masses is transposed through suitable literary conventions and incorporated into an artificial structure. Popular life is not proof, any more than the life of the élite, against the metamorphoses of art.

In one way Cohen is the exceptional case among this group of writers, since he alone has not been involved in the creative-writing schools which in recent years have proliferated in North American universities. The rest of them have all studied in such schools and have taught in them; Dave Godfrey and Robert Harlow have been heads of creative-writing departments. In the process paths have crossed in striking ways. Both Jack Hodgins and Harlow were creative-writing students of Earle Birney. It was on Birney's recommendation that Harlow went to the University of Iowa to join the celebrated Writers' Workshop there, where Godfrey and Robert Kroetsch also studied for relatively long periods.

I do not propose at this point to discuss the thorny matter of the general justification of teaching creative writing. I am sure that, after their experience as both students and teachers, none of the writers here involved would defend the argument that writing can actually be taught, that the metamorphosis of nonwriter into writer can be achieved even by the most ingenious program. Robert Harlow probably put the point as well as anyone has done when he remarked to Anthony Bukoski: "One has to teach oneself in the end. . . . However, one can manufacture a climate in which young writers can teach themselves . . . a mentor can share his experience with a young writer. . . ."[6] And if indeed the mentor has experience worth sharing, which many creative-writing teachers unfortunately lack, that is probably a helpful situation.

In fact, the kind of climate that is manufactured in creative-writing schools undoubtedly does influence the kind of writing which their alumni produce, for a number of reasons. First, the stress in such schools tends to be on craft and technique, on the artifice of writing, largely because real imagination is a rare quality and practice in the craft can at least stimulate invention. As well, the young writer who starts his career in the creative-writing school is living in an atmosphere very different from the traditional literary worlds of great cultural centres like London and Paris and New York. He is protected, for a time at least, from the need to serve an apprenticeship in literary journalism while he writes in whatever time he can spare and tries to get his work accepted by commercial publishers. The creative-writing students — and the professor-writers who earn a salary by teaching such students — are working in a setting from which the commercial imperatives are absent, a setting where the aesthetic aspects of writing have first attention and where experimentation is both affordable and encouraged. The creative-writing people have even tended to establish their own alternative publishing networks for the presentation, to whatever public may be interested, of literature that is likely to be financially unprofitable. Literary magazines — *Prism International* is a good example — are often associated with such departments; teachers in them have often taken a hand in setting up avant-garde publishing houses; and the most important books by two of the writers discussed in these essays were published by such presses — Godfrey's *The New Ancestors* by his own new press, and Harlow's *Scann* by Sono Nis Press, founded by yet another creative-writing teacher, J. Michael Yates. Given these circumstances, it is not surprising that such writers have tended to be in the vanguard of the contemporary revival of metafictional approaches.

Godfrey's *The New Ancestors* is a work of magnificent artifice and, as Michael Larsen remarks in his essay, "an achievement of intelligence."[7] While writers like Harlow and Kroetsch and Hodgins seem mainly to have accepted the examples of North

American experimental writing, Godfrey, like Leonard Cohen, has also looked back at continental European writing. With the exception of Matt Cohen's *Korsoniloff*, *The New Ancestors* is perhaps the English-Canadian novel that most clearly shows the influence of the *choseistes* who created the *nouveau roman* in France, such as Michel Butor and Alain Robbe-Grillet.

In this massive and highly populated novel set in Lost Coast, an African country resembling Ghana, where Godfrey served in CUSO, character tends to become a membrane reflecting back the impressions that flood in upon it rather than anything substantial in itself. Time is disjointed, since sequence seems unimportant in the complex of events that emerge and recede in a disparate pattern of memories. Individual episodes are viewed from multiple viewpoints, what might have been and what has been are perpetually and deliberately confused, and we are offered, as if we were reading the writer's changing mind as he works, alternative versions of events. One character dies time and time over, in different ways.

Yet out of this indeterminate flux there emerges an extraordinary panorama of Africa as an experience lived through during the years of chaos that followed the withdrawal of British imperial rule there. The vividness of the impressions comes partly from the fact that, like the *choseistes*, Godfrey is often sharply visual in his recreation of scene and action, though in this he also resembles Wyndham Lewis with his reduction of people into painterly abstractions. But it also comes from the curious and almost miragelike wavering of attention between the seer and the seen, the seer being important for his multiple perceptions of the world around him, which make up the fabric of the book, rather than for his personal qualities as a character in the traditional sense. This fact points to what, in ordinary fictional terms, must be regarded as a defect, one that *The New Ancestors* shares with the work of the *choseistes*, its lack of empathetic projection. We look outward through people's eyes; we watch their actions objectively as physical phenomena; but we do not often look back through their eyes to the beings within.

The New Ancestors is also distinctive among the novels discussed in this volume in its strong thematic structure, which stiffens the fabric of disparate perceptions and allusions. For Godfrey is a politically aware writer — almost an anti-man-of-letters in his taste for action before writing — who has been involved in Canadian nationalist movements of various kinds and is acutely conscious not only of the erosive effects of invading cultures but also of the sources of political action and political change. Politics, the politics of a land scarred and left by imperialism, is indeed the "subject" of the book, and this is why the authenticity of Godfrey's rendering of the feeling of African life at this period is so important. The privileged testimony of Audrey Thomas — another writer greatly influenced by the experience of Africa — is at this point valuable. In his essay, Larsen tells us that "Audrey Thomas, who was in Ghana when Godfrey was there, mentioned 'the shock of recognition' she felt when reading the book and discussed its fidelity to the land, to the people, and especially to 'that surreal world of rumours and counter rumours that was the last year and a half before Nkrumah was toppled by a military coup.' "[8] Like so many writers of our age from George Orwell onwards, Godfrey has understood that ideology itself is never the prime motivating factor in politics; the real motive is that sinister surrogate for sexual desire, the lust for power.

So in Godfrey we have a final arresting juxtaposition: the aesthetic view, manifest in the multiple literary and linguistic devices, and the political view, expressed in the actions and implications of *The New Ancestors*. W.H. New has described well the relationship:

> Language is not an end in itself for him, nor is the act of revolution a final answer; but the anarchy of engaging oneself with each of them can be creative. The act of writing is a political act, indissolubly bound with the culture in which it takes place.[9]

And, since Godfrey's writing about Africa takes place within the culture of Canada, we can legitimately accept a further dimension of *The New Ancestors*; that, in showing a native culture distorted by imperialism, this novel also reflects Godfrey's preoccupation with the cultural threat the United States has always posed to Canada.

There is an uncanny appropriateness, a lurking perfectionism, about everything Godfrey writes that perhaps explains why his actual volume of writing has been slight. Robert Harlow, on the other hand, falls into a pattern of flawed grandeur that is not unfamiliar among Canadian writers. Frederick Philip Grove is an obvious example in fiction and E.J. Pratt in verse. In such writers, the grasp of means does not always seem commensurate with the largeness of aims, for they are all, in scope, ambitious writers. And those who write on Harlow seem bound to contend in some way with the fact that he has not been a resounding success in terms either of acceptance by his literary peers or of popular success, despite his real merits as a writer.

Discussing Harlow's early novels, *Royal Murdoch* and *A Gift of Echoes*, W.H. New notes the quarrel within them between "realistic convention and stylistic artifice" (p. 279), and in fact throughout Harlow's fiction one finds a conflict between what I suspect is his natural desire to become a teller of rattling good tales and his sense of duty to the art-and-craft of writing. Perhaps the best expression of these divided feelings, which so many critics share about his work, has been John Moss's note on Harlow's most ambitious and undoubtedly his best novel, *Scann*, which all the commercial publishers at first rejected:

> Harlow is a first-rate craftsman whose novels seem to plummet into the abyss of obscurity between popular acceptance and critical acclaim. Only *Scann* shows resistance to the fall, but it survives more as an esoteric hybrid than as a literary masterpiece. Harlow's main problem seems to be his love of words, his passionate appetite for one hundred words where one will do. Even the most grisly or exciting scene suffers from a density of verbal obfuscation that makes it merely interesting. And he knows too much about the art of fiction: *Scann* reads like an exercise in form and technique; it is invested not with conviction but with the writer's commitment to craft; there is no passion except for Harlow's obvious desire to do things well. Yet *Scann* is an important novel, well worth the effort required to read it.[10]

Which indeed it is, for in this book there is more than the hard work and the visible chisel strokes that the earlier Harlow novels offer in their combination of conscious artifice and irrepressible honesty. It is indeed, as Louis K. MacKendrick says, "a dense, rich novel";[11] but it is also characterized by a relentless pursuit of the ultimate effect, and one cannot but agree that it is, as MacKendrick quotes Phyllis Webb saying, a work of "almost gruelling detail."[12]

But these are things that can be said about a fair number of the books that have become accepted as classics in the modernist canon. And, even if *Scann* is never likely to have a great popular appeal, it is in fact one of our best and most original examples of well-made metafiction, with the five novellas of the eccentric and scurrilous newspaperman Amory Scann united by the comments of the omniscient narrator, who represents both the novelist and, vicariously, the reader. But *Scann* is really isolated among Harlow's works — the inspired and exceptional *jeu d'esprit* of a novelist who most of the time seems a willed rather than a natural writer, achieving his workmanlike effects with a great effort which, as metafiction should, requires a corresponding effort on the reader's part. Perhaps the clue lies in MacKendrick's remark that "Harlow's own influence is as a teacher, not as a novelist."[13] His intense and transmissible concern for the craft of writing in fact masks an imaginative unsureness that most of the time satisfies neither of his potential audiences, and prevents him from being either a critical or a popular success on any broad scale.

Jack Hodgins is a preeminently natural writer, and one feels that the creative-writing schools have been unable to help or harm him to any great extent. His fluent prose, his vivid and convincingly visual imagery, his ever-inventive fantasy, his sheer sense of literary atmospherics, more than compensate for the lapses of proportion and the occasional jarring concatenations that a writer more self-consciously dominated by the canons of his craft might have avoided.

I have already written in *Canadian Literature* and in *Saturday Night* on this aspect of Hodgins' work, and David Jeffrey — the author of the essay on him in *Canadian Writers and Their Works* — chooses to disagree with me. There is certainly a difference of attitude between us on the point of self-consistency: how far the mood of a book can be disrupted and its credibility (which is something different from the plausibility of realism) be retained. My argument is that with the introduction of larger-than-life grotesques, like the cult-leader Keneally in *The Invention of the World*, or portentous bores like the poet Joseph Bourne in *The Resurrection of Joseph Bourne*, into what on Jeffrey's admission are novels of "painterly realism," Hodgins weakens the very fabric of his fiction in ways that contrast sharply with the practice of actual painterly realists like Alex Colville, who figure the extraordinary through an intensely focused perception of the ordinary, and so set the imagination to lively work. This is what, in words quoted by Jeffrey, Hodgins claims to be his intent: "The act of writing to me is an attempt to shine a light on that ocean and those trees so bright that we can see right through them to the reality that is constant."[14] And this, I have contended, is precisely what he does best; it is the inward luminosity of Hodgins' novels that makes them so distinctive, not the central characters inflated into strange balloon figures that lurch heavily about them rather like Gargantua, if one could imagine him in a flowery and lucent Pre-Raphaelite landscape.

There is always, of course, room for differences of critical interpretation, particularly in a series of volumes like *Canadian Writers and Their Works*, whose spirit has never been less than "let a hundred flowers blossom and a hundred schools of thought contend," but this hardly seems to justify the style of argument Jeffrey uses — virtually the *argumentum ad hominem* — as he attempts to dismiss my contentions, not by logic, but by labelling: he says that I am "typically affirmative of social realism (perhaps especially in the British vein)," and he accuses me of applying "a strict and almost unmetaphorical nineteenth-century brand of realist criterion."[15]

All this is unfounded. I have never even been sure what "social realism" (as distinct from *socialist* realism, which I abhor) really is; I have never used the term since the day in 1948 when Herbert Read, who was one of my close critical associates in Britain and far from a realist of any kind, said to me: "What do you mean by social realism? All realism is social since it deals with the relations between men, and so is all literature."

I have always held, in any case, that for a critic to accept labels or to think in categories or to establish petty orthodoxies is self-defeating, a negation of the critic's duty to receive and perceive freely. If Jeffrey had taken the trouble to read my statement of critical principles in *Odysseus Ever Returning*, he would hardly be accusing me so hastily of promoting "a strict . . . nineteenth-century brand of realist criterion," just as if he had read my essays on modern French and classic Russian writers he would hardly be accusing me of being "especially in the British vein." He may have read his Hodgins; he has obviously not read his Woodcock, and by the misinterpretation of a couple of isolated passages has led himself into some untenable assumptions.

Often, in such situations, the disputants are nearer to each other than immediately appears; genuine misunderstanding, or critical sectarianism, obscures a basic agreement. The particular passage in which I refer to Hodgins and to which Jeffrey takes exception projects a view of the novelist that — when one relates his own remarks to those of the critics of whom he seems to approve — is not far from the position Jeffrey himself appears to hold.

Let us look at what I actually said; in discussing it, we may gain some enlightenment not only on Woodcock, but also on Hodgins. I began by confirming from my own experience of life on Vancouver Island the experiential truth of Hodgins' projection of the eccentric human community that in the mid-nineteenth century came into being there, on one of the last of the last frontiers. Then, criticizing Hodgins' metamorphosis of the real-life Brother Twelve into the fictionally false prophet Keneally, "a semi-supernatural being of malign and magical powers," I remarked:

> For what he is doing is to juxtapose true myth with fabricated myth. The strange life of the Vancouver Island community is one of those natural gifts to the novelist — truth grown so much stranger than fiction that in memory it is already myth, even before it is set down on paper. To add further convolutions is to transfer it into the world of fictional invention, and to lose it as mythic truth.[16]

In trying to equate this eminently Proustian view with what he somewhat archaically calls social realism, Jeffrey fails to pick the essential clues: I am talking of the transforming power of memory that turns fact into myth; I am talking about myth and the self-consistency of myth, not about actuality; I am posing a kind of realism that denies naturalism in the same way as it questions those extremities of artifice where invention takes over from imagination and the link with reality, as distinct from actuality, is weakened.

All this, I suggest, is not far from the image of the essential Hodgins that Jeffrey projects. Trying to define Hodgins' work,

Jeffrey speaks of "romantic realism" or "romantic pastoral comedy," and he quotes W.J. Keith, who describes Hodgins as "a regional writer in the most profound sense of that term: he transforms his local backyard into the image of the whole created universe."[17] Precisely the Blakean point that I have always been making about Hodgins: that the backyard transformed is sufficient to mirror forth "the whole created universe." This view, in fact, Jeffrey himself seems to accept when, later in his essay, he says: "This surely is the reality for which Hodgins himself so vigorously strives – the literal world suddenly seen as for the first time and then recognized not only for its husk of externality but for its vital inner spirit — without which there is hardly any meaning for the world at all."[18] But if that literal inner world is seen according to its "vital inner spirit," surely the intrusion of outer spirits (outer in the sense of being out of tune like Keneally) must destroy its self-consistency. And, in his own oblique way, Jeffrey does acknowledge this when, referring to a review I wrote of *The Resurrection of Joseph Bourne*, he remarks: "Whereas Woodcock concentrates on the title character of Joseph Bourne, finding him a bit flat (he is), he misses that the real hero of the novel in Hodgins' formulation is the *community*, Port Annie."[19] This of course is an admission of the extent to which Hodgins is a regional novelist, concerned primarily with communities and their "vital inner spirits." And I concentrated my criticism on the character of the senilely eccentric poet Bourne precisely because the way Hodgins portrayed him distracted our attention from the "community," the real *subject* of the novel. Essentially we agree; the overinflated Brocken spectres that haunt Hodgins' novels lead one away from the real direction of the book, which is towards the romantic apprehension of a frontier world, meaning by that not only a world on the far edge of human settlement, but also a world where the edge of human experience touches a deeper reality.

Jeffrey has rightly remarked that Hodgins — unlike other novelists discussed in this volume — "bears the character less of a deconstructionist than a constructionist."[20] As I have suggested in my criticism, the tendency towards deconstruction is there, but Hodgins' vision is essentially a pastorally comic one, and as such, in its principal manifestation, benign and ultimately ordered. This is perhaps why in the end one is more satisfied by his stories than by his novels, since in the former the order that derives from the writer's neo-Platonic vision of the role of art is not dislocated.

In his inclination towards fantasy and his departures from the verisimilitude that is the aim of ordinary realism, Hodgins resembles the other novelists discussed in this volume. His fiction differs from theirs in that at its best it offers the romantic illusion of being natural. One tastes the atmosphere of his novels; one can visualize them credibly; one finds his minor characters at least believable if eccentric; one appreciates – and on this Jeffrey and I agree — his sense of community as a living element in fiction. Of course, there is artifice in his writing, but the artifice does not dominate, as it tends to do in the work of the other novelists here discussed, and nowhere more than in the books of Robert Kroetsch.

Of all the writers included in this collection, Kroetsch has been the boldest and the most experimental in his advances into metafiction. His evolution from the comparative realism of his first novel, *But We Are Exiles*, through the growing detachment of his comedy from actual life and its steady mythification is a fascinating one, well delineated by Peter Thomas in his essay,[21] which does raise the problem of how far we are to regard Kroetsch as a writer concerned entirely with the game of literature, and how far we are to detect in his novels a didactic constituent.

I do not think any of Kroetsch's critics or his intelligent readers would be inclined to dispute Frank Davey's suggestion that in his novels one encounters one of the most "powerful" expressions in Canadian writing of the "sense of a fragmentary, chaotic universe," as absurd as that of Malraux or Camus.[22] The point at issue is whether there is some kind of message of regeneration to be read in the novels, or whether in their progression of parody and self-parody they take one into an auto-reflexive world that leads reductively to a kind of nihilism of art preying on rather than being sustained by art.

As Davey, writing when Kroetsch had completed the triptych of *The Words of My Roaring*, *The Studhorse Man*, and *Gone Indian*, but before *Badlands* appeared in 1975, notes:

All four of Kroetsch's novels deliver partially crippled men from failure by means of cataclysmic immersion in natural process — particularly in carnality, passion, and death. Tragic-comic in tone, and comic in structure, they find in the "green world" of the wild northern landscape and of unbridled human sexuality the healing forces which can counteract the paralytic effects of a pragmatic, mechanized culture and thus return meaning and joy to individual life."[23]

On the other hand, writing with the same time-limited viewpoint, W.H. New — in the second edition of *Literary History of Canada* — seems to sense the way in which Kroetsch's concern for the actual process of writing, with its elaborate play of ways of seeing and speaking, would undermine any moral structure just as, through its essential ambiguity, ". . . 'myths' like the Golden West and the Canadian Mosaic are both celebrated and challenged" (p. 280). Of *Gone Indian*, the last novel in the triptych, New says:

> If Jeremy Sadness, the central Manhattan-born character who "dreamed northwest," seems lost and inarticulate in his quest, that is part of Kroetsch's aim. As in *The Studhorse Man*, the characters' identities are given by his fictional techniques into the hands of another. People narrate other people's lives, and so redraw them. The process of being absorbed into another's dream utters an alienation of a profound and horrifying kind, which is only intensified by the brittle sexual wit that marks the trilogy's surface. The cultural overtones they carry, moreover, related Kroetsch's books closely to those of Atwood and Godfrey; a *way of saying* implicitly establishes *a way of knowing*, and if these processes are surrendered to others, that which is distinctive about them no longer survives. (pp. 280–81)

New still emphasizes the "intense realization of region" in Kroetsch's novels (p. 281), an aspect Thomas tends to regard as somewhat apart from Kroetsch's involvement in the fictitiousness of fiction, in its inevitable tendency, once the demands of realism are relaxed, towards self-reflexiveness. In his comment on *The Studhorse Man*, he shows how Kroetsch, seeming to be more regional by adopting native Canadian myths of the Trickster in preference to the Odyssean myths that tended to dominate his earlier fiction, has in fact moved farther away from life into literature:

Both *But We Are Exiles* and *The Words of My Roaring* maintain an uneasy pact with formal realism, with verisimilitude. The measure of *The Studhorse Man* is its very fictitiousness; it is a game with character, scene, development, point of view, and the metamorphic principle itself. The novel succeeds when we allow its exuberance and grant the assumption that fixed structures, once recognized, are, by definition, limits to imaginative freedom. The artist, too, is a Trickster, dodging irresponsibly between the genres which he has inherited and with which his reader is familiar. His task is to convert and invert the structures and symbols we know too well, to insist that literary form is forever in the making. And his primary reference is to other narrative structures, not to "life."[24]

Literary deconstructionism, of which Kroetsch is the most distinguished practitioner among contemporary Canadian novelists, leads inevitably to a retreat into the realms where life cannot even fulfil its traditional aestheticist role of imitating art because art has created its own life, its own plausibility beyond the limits of verisimilitude. It is a process often repeated in the history of literature, perhaps most strikingly in the Joycean progression from *Dubliners* through *Ulysses* to *Finnegans Wake*. But Kroetsch's deconstructionism is in a way more open than Joyce's. Its rejection of a logically consistent aesthetic means that even the literal is not to be excluded, and life and the concern for life emerge and re-emerge in his novels, so that *Badlands*, for all its tall-telling rejection of probability is, as Thomas remarks, both "humanistic and remote." Thomas regards *What the Crow Said* as a "fearsomely reductive book, bleak and even desperate at the core," and concerning the end of the novel he remarks: "The seduction of silence, the brotherhood of death, the fall into a void of insignificance, a biography of divided identity, self-love and excrement — this is the most savage reduction of any heroic image of man."[25]

But Thomas also rightly recognizes that the Trickster role of the artist is one based on the acceptance of self-contradiction; that in following the reductive directions of aestheticism to their very end, Kroetsch is giving us an oblique warning not to allow the formal processes of art to make us lose sight of the fact that humanity still lies at the heart of fiction, its necessary core. And so perhaps Davey in a way is right in his view of Kroetsch, and Thomas also in his question:

Where does he go now? He has dropped us where the outhouse stood. He must be tempted, working by contraries as he does, to wash us clean again at the springs of renewal.²⁶

Which is as it should be, for, by however many indirections, the content of literature comes from life, just as its language is derived from the speech of people in the real world, and both must return at times to the wells of experience.

NOTES

¹ Linda Hutcheon, "Leonard Cohen and His Works," in *Canadian Writers and Their Works*, ed. Robert Lecker, Jack David, and Ellen Quigley, Fiction ser., x (Toronto: ECW, 1989), p. 32; hereafter cited as *CWTW*.

² *CWTW*, Fiction ser., x, p. 28.

³ *CWTW*, Fiction ser., x, p. 25.

⁴ Quoted in Michael Ondaatje, *Leonard Cohen*, New Canadian Library, Canadian Writers Series, No. 5 (Toronto: McClelland and Stewart, 1970), p. 45.

⁵ *CWTW*, Fiction ser., x, p. 41.

⁶ Quoted in Anthony Bukoski, "The Canadian Writer and the Iowa Experience," *Canadian Literature*, No. 101 (Summer 1984), p. 17.

⁷ *CWTW*, Fiction ser., x, p. 100.

⁸ "The Smell of Recognition," rev. of *The New Ancestors, Canadian Literature*, No. 49 (Summer 1971), p. 78.

⁹ W.H. New, "Fiction," in *Literary History of Canada: Canadian Literature in English*, 2nd ed., gen. ed. and introd. Carl F. Klinck (Toronto: Univ. of Toronto Press, 1976), III, 283. All further references to this work appear in the text.

¹⁰ John Moss, "Harlow, Robert," in *A Reader's Guide to the Canadian Novel* (Toronto: McClelland and Stewart, 1981), p. 118.

¹¹ *CWTW*, Fiction ser., x, p. 147.

¹² Phyllis Webb, rev. of *Scann, Critics on Air*, CBC Radio, 2 Dec. 1972 (FM), 4 Dec. 1972 (AM).

¹³ *CWTW*, Fiction ser., x, p. 130.

¹⁴ Geoff Hancock, "An Interview with Jack Hodgins," *Canadian Fiction Magazine*, Nos. 32–33 (1979–80), p. 47.

¹⁵ *CWTW*, Fiction ser., x, p. 200.

¹⁶ George Woodcock, "Novels from Near and Far," rev. of *The Invention*

of the World, and four other books, *Canadian Literature,* No. 73 (Summer 1977), pp. 90–91. See also my "Among the Remnants of Hippiedom," rev. of *The Resurrection of Joseph Bourne, Saturday Night,* Oct. 1979, pp. 70, 72.

[17] W.J. Keith, "Jack Hodgins's Island World," rev. of *The Barclay Family Theatre, The Canadian Forum,* Sept.–Oct. 1981, p. 31.

[18] *CWTW,* Fiction ser., x, p. 224.

[19] Cf. R.P. Bilan, rev. of *The Resurrection of Joseph Bourne,* in "Letters in Canada 1979: Fiction," *University of Toronto Quarterly,* 49 (Summer 1980), 331–33.

[20] *CWTW,* Fiction ser., x, p. 204.

[21] *CWTW,* Fiction ser., x, p. 243.

[22] Frank Davey, "Robert Kroetsch," in *From There to Here: A Guide to English-Canadian Literature since 1960* (Erin, Ont.: Porcépic, 1974), p. 155.

[23] Davey, p. 158.

[24] Peter Thomas, "Robert Kroetsch and His Works," in *CWTW,* Fiction ser., x, p. 271.

[25] *CWTW,* Fiction ser., x, p. 289.

[26] *CWTW,* Fiction ser., x, p. 289.